DARE
—— TO ——
BELIEVE

My Journey out of Homosexuality

ROBIN T.

Printed in the United States of America

ISBN Paperback: 978-0-578-54051-1
ISBN eBook: 978-0-578-54052-8

Cover and Interior Design: Ghislain Viau

"So if the Son sets you free, you will be free indeed."
(John 8:36 ESV)

In memory of Uncle Wesley;
a good man with a kind and generous heart.

Many thanks to Ann, Tom, Dorthea, Judy, Steve, Margaret,
Andrew, Susan and Ted for their editing contributions.
(It took a village.)

Above all, praise and adoration to the great Hound of
Heaven! He never gave up on me, though I gave Him every
reason to do just that. May His name be exalted and
glorified by the words on these pages.

CONTENTS

Introduction. 1

1. Why I Write 5

2. Marriage. 11

3. Repent. 19

4. Changing My Mind 25

5. Unbound 37

6. Shepherd's Group 51

7. Theophostic 63

8. Catholicism 77

9. Therapy 95

10. Dad 103

11. Mom 121

12. Mother. 135

13. Gender Identity Confusion. 151

14. In Search of a Family. 163

15. The Wonder of Salt 177

Dear Reader,

While my thoughts on homosexuality are orthodox, my writing style is anything but. One of the reasons I have decided to depart from a traditional writing style is because I want you to feel as if we are sitting at your kitchen table sipping tea while I tell you my story. In order to pull this off I have added many side remarks in parentheses. Everything in italics is an unspoken prayer or thought. Sometimes they will be in parentheses and other times, not.

I have also chosen to write in this manner to lighten things up a bit. My story gets heavy at times and hopefully a little humor will get you through it. (It certainly did me.) But do take heart—it has a really happy ending.

So, God be with you—may your heart be touched—and I hope there's a little laughter mingled in with the tears.

In Jesus Love,

INTRODUCTION

Writing a book is not the easiest thing to do and perhaps that is why many people who have a story to tell never get around to putting it down on paper. I often wonder if folks who crank out one best seller after another were born with a specific writer's gene. If that's the case, I arrived on the planet without this being part of my DNA. Though I've had moments of overwhelming inspiration where the words have poured out of me, there are other times when writing has been toilsome. For the most part, this book has been the latter; downright excruciating! I have asked myself many times if that's a sign that the Lord is not in this endeavor—that I'm writing simply for my own catharsis. Still, in the depths of my soul I feel compelled to share my story with others. So maybe the fact that I have crawled along at a snail's pace—revising chapters again and again, is more indicative that there are forces of evil doing their best to keep me from doing so.

As you've probably gathered from the title of this book you now hold in your hands, my subject matter is very controversial. I'm ever so mindful of the fact that if I don't say things just right, I'll be the cause of folks being rushed to the ER with their blood pressure through the roof! That has me quite concerned because honestly, the odds of my sharing this story in a way that will have the masses cheering are slim to none. Non-believers will undoubtedly think I am delusional. That's to be expected. Though it will hurt my feelings when the name calling becomes brutal, God will give me grace to handle being referred to as a demented, hateful old hag. But the sad reality is that many of my brothers and sisters in Christ will agree with them and that will be a bitter pill to swallow.

Please believe me when I tell you that I have fervently sought to know the truth. For almost a decade now I have been asking God over and over again if my thoughts and opinions are wrong. Am I missing the boat? Perhaps I'm just being stubborn, narrow-minded, arrogant and totally bullheaded in advocating something that the vast majority of folks on the planet vehemently oppose. Truth be told there are deacons, ministers, pastors, priests, radio talk show hosts and others of distinguished reputations who would say, "Yes" to all of the above. Many of them are older and wiser than I. They outrank me in status, have more education, better careers, drive nicer cars, live in fancier houses and have been to Disneyland. Many of them have memorized more Bible verses than I have and for sure have a much better grasp of theology.

While there are some who may feel I might be on to something, many of those same folks will still contend it's time to move on because we've lost the battle on this issue. I'm well aware of the fact that for the sake of peace it would be better to accept what is, leave well enough alone and refrain from rattling the beehive. Even the people I worship with Sunday after Sunday are all over the map on this topic. While there are some who will respond with an enthusiastic "Amen" to what I have to say, others will be downright annoyed with me! As I push this issue front and center it may not bode well for oneness of spirit. In fact, I may very well end up being responsible for one great big church brawl. (Not cool!)

In light of all of this, the obvious question is this; "Why even bother to write?" That's a fair enough question and I believe I have a good enough answer.

Chapter 1

WHY I WRITE

For a very long time, I was trapped in homosexual sin. I referred to myself as 'gay' for most of my adult life, even though my life was anything but. Being an active homosexual was more like being the star of a daytime soap. Did I believe I was born a homosexual? No, I didn't. And the fact that I never went there—that was rather strange to me. Truth be told, for all the years spent on the wrong side of the railroad tracks, I had no idea why I fell in love with women and not men. For me, it was one of the great mysteries of the universe. But when all was said and done, I decided that it simply didn't matter. For whatever reason, I accepted this to be my personal reality and anyone that tried to suggest otherwise was the enemy (who I avoided like the plague)!

I had my first homosexual relationship at the age of 19, although I had been falling in love with women since junior high school. On my 54th birthday, when relationship #12 derailed, I told the Lord I was done. I fessed up that He had been right and for 35 years I had been terribly wrong. My resolve that morning was to never again engage in homosexual behavior. Little did I know Jesus had so much more in store for me. His plan was not only to free me from the behavior but also from the desires and attractions.

It appears that in general, Christians are more comfortable with repentant homosexuals who identify as Same-Sex Attracted (SSA) than with those who claim complete deliverance from every aspect of homosexuality. The SSA person who is committed to a celibate life is held in high regard and seen as heroic—perhaps even virtuous. Remaining sexually pure when all the forces around you are shouting, "IT'S OKAY TO BE GAY!" is no small challenge and for the record—I wholeheartedly agree! So, hats off, kudos and high fives to those who are honoring the Lord with their bodies. On the other hand, if your story is one of total healing and transformation—you are viewed as an outlier, rare exception and possibly even held in suspicion. Were you really even gay? Perhaps you're only on sabbatical and in time the desires will be back. Or maybe you're not telling the truth because after all, how do you change something that just plain is?

One purpose in writing this book is to take folks down the road to recovery in which Jesus led me along. As I detail this journey I will not be referring to myself as SSA. Surprisingly I had not even heard of this updated terminology until several years into my recovery. Being 'out of the loop', or as some would say, 'out to lunch', was a blessing in disguise. I had no idea that my homosexual attractions/desires had been reclassified as an 'affliction' and need not be seriously dealt with. For some reason unbeknownst to me, that email never reached my inbox. I was under the assumption I needed to repent and nail every aspect of homosexuality to the foot of the cross as it was all sinful and offensive to God. I didn't know if I would ever be completely free from homosexual thoughts and feelings but early on, I was 100% committed to warring against them whenever they showed up.

The Bible comes down very hard on homosexuality. Unfortunately, many folks have been crushed in spirit as they have had Bible verses shouted at them. This may explain in part why there has been a concerted effort to move away from Biblical terminology, derived from verses considered too harsh, unloving and just plain outdated. While it's true that Scripture's straightforward condemnation of homosexuality is a tad brutal, it pales in comparison to the great hope of deliverance spelled out in God's Word to those who turn away from sin. "And such were some of you. But you were washed, you were sanctified, you were justified in the name of the Lord Jesus Christ and by the Spirit of our God" (1 Corinthians 6:11 ESV).

For me personally, keeping the terminology Biblical made it easier not to miss out on this glorious truth. So even though Same-Sex Attraction means the same thing as Homosexual Attraction, I shall refrain from using the updated reclassification. It's possible that folks prefer to identify as SSA because it is not condemned in the pages of Scripture. True enough. In fact, it's not even mentioned. While it may provide a neutral, safe place, free from a label that has been shaming and stigmatizing—in my opinion, there's a downside to changing the language. Because there's no mention of SSA anywhere in the Bible, there's also no hope given anywhere in the pages of Scripture promising freedom from it. This may seem silly and even ridiculous because I keep hearing from folks that the Bible only condemns homosexual behavior—not the desire and attraction. Nonetheless, for me to desire something that put nails in Jesus' hands and feet, that God refers to as "an abomination"—well—that seemed sinful as well. First Corinthians 6:11 held out a glorious promise of complete transformation. In my mind that meant freedom from homosexual everything. Undoubtedly, in saying this I will annoy some and have others reaching for their pain meds. Please know that getting on everyone's last nerve is not one of my goals in writing this book.

"So," you may ask, "If the goal in writing is not to irritate all who read this, why bother putting on paper a message that will do just that?"

Here's the reason why. I made a promise to the Lord. "I have not refrained my lips, O Lord, thou knowest. I have not hid thy righteousness within my heart; I have declared thy faithfulness and thy salvation: I have not concealed thy lovingkindness and thy truth from the great congregation" (Psalm 40:9b-10 KJV). As God grants opportunity, I freely share the amazing thing He has done. "He brought me up also out of an horrible pit, out of the miry clay, and set my feet upon a rock, and established my goings" (Psalm 40:2 KJV). I've been telling this story for close to a decade and still feel the same excitement I felt the first time I proclaimed this awesome news. Although my one-on-one encounters are much easier for me than writing an entire book, I felt the Lord would have me to do this as well, in fulfillment of this promise made.

In my travels I have spoken with countless persons who love someone who identifies as homosexual. Often, they are parents—heartsick over their sons' and daughters' choices. I write this book for all of you whose situation this is. My soul's desire is to give you hope and encouragement. Your prayers are powerful; don't ever doubt that. And come the day your loved one wants out of the trap they are in, you'll have the roadmap to point them in the right direction. Granted, this isn't the only path to freedom. There are other powerful ministries out there besides the ones I will be mentioning in the chapters to come. The message of this book is certainly not **This way and no other!** I just felt it best to only share what I experienced. I can vouch for the effectiveness of those ministries and say with total conviction they were mightily effective in bringing about a transformational healing.

We live in crazy times. Up is down, black is white, true is false, good is bad and sinful behavior is cause for a parade. One's sexual orientation is set in cement and can never be changed. Your gender, however, which is determined by chromosomes, is something that can be tampered with and absolutely should be reassigned if you've determined God somehow goofed up by putting you in the wrong body. (*I really have lived too long. Come, Lord Jesus!*) All this insanity brings me to my final reason for writing this book. I feel compelled to speak truth amid the lies. This is something I've done day in and day out for quite some time now and yet the conversations are usually brief as not much can be said standing in line at the grocery store or walking to cars after seeing a movie. Oh yes, I can take the conversation to 'freedom and deliverance' in a hot second with total strangers if there's the slightest opening. But I never get to tell my entire story. So, I'm writing it all down in this book to set the record straight (no pun intended).

Please remember as you read this book, I am telling **my** story and therefore will be talking about how the Lord changed **my** life. This topic is very explosive and it would only add fuel to the fire to write about the ills of others. My plan is to keep the focus on my own transgressions and errors (which will give me plenty of material to work with). That's the good news. The not so good news is that in doing so I'll be using some form of me, my and I in every sentence—which will lead everyone to conclude I'm one of the biggest egomaniacs on the planet. If that's all I get accused of, I'll be getting off easy.

God alone knows what awaits me. But no matter what lies ahead, I'm going to dare to write about what God can do in the life of a broken, wounded sinner such as I. The deepest desire of my heart is that someone will dare to believe it's true.

Chapter 2

MARRIAGE

On June 26th, 2015 marriage between persons of the same gender became legal in all fifty states, compliments of the Supreme Court. Many in the country celebrated while others lamented the continuation of our moral decay. Sadly, it appears that lines have now been drawn in the sand with those opposed to homosexual marriage on one side and those for it on the other. Even worse, we find ourselves with yet another issue dividing us—not only in the secular realm but tragically also in our churches.

Surprisingly, even in the heyday of my 'not-so-gay days', I was not a proponent of homosexual marriage. It was not on my list of issues to go to battle over because I felt marriage was something that heterosexual folks did. Yes, it amazes even me that though in the depths of iniquity which skewed my moral judgments, my thoughts on marriage remained Biblically intact. However, that did not mean I wasn't in favor of homosexuals being in legally-protected, committed relationships, because I was. My thinking was that we too were entitled to a special day where vows were exchanged, a big party followed, and everyone came bearing gifts. I very much longed for that moment in time. I just didn't want to call it marriage.

Since walking away from my sinful past and being transformed by the power of God, I have become a huge proponent of marriage. As far as I'm concerned, there is nothing more amazing than a loving, Christ-centered marriage. I'm in awe of folks who have joyfully walked together for decades—faithfully honoring the commitment they made to one another. Honestly, my greatest heartache in life is that I missed out on this. The only thing that consoles me is knowing I spared a husband and children much heartache and pain. I was so messed up, I would have destroyed my marriage, severely wounding a hubby and kids. I don't think I could have endured the guilt and shame had I done such a thing to my family. I can hardly handle the remorse I feel over hurting former partners with whom I formed illegitimate unions.

Yet, I longed to be loved. In all my 35 years of trudging in the muck and mire, that's all I ever wanted—to be in a committed relationship with another human being who would walk life's journey with me 'til death did us part. My soul, however, was so broken I thought my only option for finding such a relationship would be with another woman. Although not a very good Bible student back then, I knew enough that as a follower of Jesus Christ, this was not an option. God's

Word clearly ruled out any possibility of a homosexual union ever becoming a reality in my life.

Often, I would lament, *How come you're being so unfair, Lord? What's the big deal if I love another woman? Isn't love always a good thing?*

Both of my sisters were married, and I remember one holiday after another, sitting quietly by myself, observing them lovin' on their husbands, knowing I would never experience the marital bliss that was playing out before my eyes. It was extremely painful, and I eventually moved far away, coming home less and less to avoid the depression it plunged me into.

For most of my twenties I vacillated between two opposing opinions (of which neither was true). **Opinion A:** God was mean and cruel to forbid me being with another woman. And then there was **Opinion B:** The Bible meant something other than what was clearly written, therefore I could be a Christian in good standing with God if I engaged in the right kind of homosexual behavior. When I was twenty-eight I made a tragic decision. I opted to go with **Opinion B.** In a state of delusion (which lasted decades) I decided the homosexuality condemned in Scripture didn't really pertain to me and thus gave myself permission to disobey and distort His Word (being in total denial, of course, that this was what I was doing). Well, the results were devastating. As it turns out, God actually did mean what He wrote. (Imagine that!) But what I know now that I didn't know 40 years ago is that all those verses forbidding homosexual unions weren't put in the Bible because the Lord God is a heartless tyrant who has nothing better to do than to rain on our parades and make us miserable. Quite the contrary. They are there because He loves us and knows what's best for the humans He created. When He forbids something, it's for our protection and ultimate good. Back then it was a bitter pill to swallow so I rebelled by deciding I knew best (which was not a very smart move on my part). Completely disregarding warnings such as, "Woe to those who are wise in their own eyes and clever in their own sight" (Isaiah 5:21 NIV), I went off on my merry way, completely oblivious to the peril awaiting me. Now, many years later, after suffering through numerous consequences brought about from a defiant spirit, I stand on this undeniable truth: God created men to love women and for women to love them back. "Therefore a man shall leave his father and his mother and hold fast to his wife, and they shall become one flesh" (Genesis 2:24 ESV). Jesus quoted this verse when answering a question posed by the Pharisees concerning divorce (Mark 10:7).

The design for marriage between one man and one woman is recorded in both testaments, ruling out any other options. One man, one woman, period. There are no loopholes, amendments or revisions offered by the Lord. Instead, He reiterates that this was the plan at the very beginning and is how it will be until we all get to heaven, where there will be no marriage. In saying this, my heart goes out to every person with homosexual longings. I know how difficult it is to hear this pronouncement and almost impossible to accept—especially when God created us for intimacy and partnership, knowing it wasn't good for us to be alone. God established the institution of marriage for this very reason: "It is not good that the man should be alone; I will make him a helper fit for him" (Genesis 2:18 ESV). I have come to accept that my longing for a spouse was part of my spiritual DNA. But the way I acted it out was a sign that my soul was very messed up and badly broken. Some folks can actually handle being single, but for me, the thought of life without a mate felt like a dagger in my heart.

Perhaps my feelings of gloom and doom were intensified due to the fact I was so deeply wounded by my parents' divorce. I was seven years old when my father left. To survive this devastation, I came up with a plan to combat the depression that was consuming me. Granted, being just shy of the third grade, it's not like I woke up one morning, pulled out my journal and started writing. But as I look back on that moment in time, that's exactly what I was doing. One afternoon I hopped on my bike and rode over to the schoolyard swing set, where I did all my serious thinking. As I swung back and forth on the swings I vowed to be married, with children, by the time I was twenty-one. I'd then have a family of my own to replace the one that had been taken from me. (Obviously that plan involved marrying in junior high school so my kids would all be in tow by the target date.) Although my future plans didn't completely dissolve all the sadness consuming my heart, the thought of once again being part of an intact family unit kept me afloat. But by the time I reached my 21st birthday I realized my feelings for men were null and void. Thus, my dreams for the big church wedding with a happily-ever-after ending went up in smoke. Instead of planning a wedding and honeymoon, my energy was spent battling forces pulling me into that which I knew to be sin. A constant reading of Leviticus 18 and Romans 1 kept me walking the straight and narrow for many years. But it did little to quell my soul's cry for partnership and family with a woman. Thus, feeling destined to be single 'til the end of time I tried to encourage myself with advice from the apostle Paul on the benefits of flying solo. "Yet those who marry will have worldly troubles, and I would spare you that" (1 Corinthians 7:28b ESV). "And the unmarried or betrothed woman is anxious about the things of the Lord, how to be holy in body and spirit" (1 Corinthians 7:34b ESV). "So then he who marries his betrothed does well, and he who refrains from marriage will do even better" (1 Corinthians 7:38 ESV).

But even after reading how being unmarried affords one many perks, my heart never stopped wanting to be one flesh with someone I was in love with. Many times I asked the Lord, *Oh, dear Jesus, what is wrong with me? Why can't I be like the Apostle Paul?*

The answer to that question was also to be found in 1 Corinthians 7, but somehow I overlooked it. "I wish that all were as I myself am. But each has his own gift from God, one of one kind and one of another" (1 Corinthians 7:7 ESV). The gift being referred to by Paul is celibacy. There actually are folks who have been given the gift of celibacy and who also prefer singleness to partnership. For the record, I'm not one of them. I love passion, togetherness, companionship and being in each other's space. I want the chaos and drama that occurs when folks in a covenant relationship are living together under one roof in close quarters. Yet with that being said, I am finally at peace with my status as a single gal. The Lord's faithfulness and steadfast love continually sustain me.

Yes, God's grace is sufficient in that I have been given strength enough to live a productive, meaningful life, though different from the one I was gifted for. For this I truly am grateful and even a little amazed that for the most part, I'm relatively happy—even during seasons of loneliness. But I still sometimes lament having missed out on marriage. There have been moments when I've imagined myself on my wedding day— exchanging vows with the man I love—friends and family gathered to say the "Amen!" (Most of them would be shouting it.) I'm quite certain it would be the happiest day of my life. (*Hmmm.*) Even when just dreaming about it, I feel an emotional surge of wonderment and joy. What would that have been like?

So, now that I've divulged this unfulfilled desire of my heart, which some will find to be completely preposterous, another question that needs to be answered is, "What happened to the gal who was so crazy about women?" If you're serious about wanting to know the answer to that inquiry, keep reading. To the rest of you skeptics who have already judged my credibility suspect and my sanity on a permanent vacation, well why don't you keep reading too? Oh, come on. I dare you.

Chapter 3

REPENT

We live in a day ruled by political correctness. The list of things considered offensive grows longer by the minute. Hurting someone's feelings has become a social felony, punishable by being branded with labels that could very well ruin your reputation. This has resulted in Christians doing their best to refrain from using Biblical words that might rile folks up. Thus, many churches have decided that having worship services that are 'seeker friendly' is more productive than for lost souls to squirm in their seats under the conviction of the Holy Spirit. Archaic, outdated, shaming words such as **sin, Satan, hell, judgment**, and the like are used less and less—except by a few staunch, old-school fundamentalists who just can't seem to get with the program. They, however, are themselves growing old and before too much longer will be leaving the planet to go be with the Lord. Once that happens, it will be safe for everyone to come out of hiding as churches will become even more focused on helping us feel good about ourselves.

Things were much, much different when I entered into my first homosexual relationship. All those dreadful words that today are taboo were fully operational and used ad nauseum. One Biblical term I did my best to turn a deaf ear to as I became more entrenched in homosexual sin was the word **repent**. Once upon a time, that Biblical word was a regular part of most every Christian's consciousness and vocabulary because we heard it from the pulpit on a regular basis. And while I was reading the Bible off and on throughout my years in captivity, I only saw what I wanted to see, turning a blind eye to everything else that would have caused me to squirm. I did, though happen to notice that both John the Baptist and the Apostle Paul preached on repentance. John the Baptist cried, "Repent, for the kingdom of heaven is at hand" (Matthew 3:2 ESV). The apostle Paul spoke the following to those with whom he had an audience: "The times of ignorance God overlooked, but now he commands all people everywhere to repent" (Acts 17:30 ESV). But in my depravity I wrote them both off as 'unloving' and thus felt perfectly within my right to turn a deaf ear—giving little, if any, credence to their words. There was also Peter to contend with. He also preached on repentance. As many times as I had read the book of Acts, it escaped me that he concluded his very first sermon with "Repent and be baptized every one of you in the name of Jesus Christ for the forgiveness of your sins, and you will receive the gift of the Holy Spirit" (Acts 2:38 ESV). (Hard to admit how many years that went right over my head.) But the clearest indication of my being spiritually comatose was how I completely overlooked all the emphasis Jesus placed on repentance. He kicked off His public ministry with, "Repent, for the kingdom of heaven is at hand" (Matthew 4:17 ESV). That was the message He gave the twelve when He sent them out two by two, "So they went out and proclaimed that people should repent" (Mark 6:12 ESV). And in the final book of the Bible, The Revelation, Jesus was still on point. He dictated letters to the seven churches of Asia Minor through the Apostle John. Turns out most of those churches were pretty messed up as the Lord found fault with five of the assemblies. His message to each of them concluded with, "Repent!" (Revelation 2:5, 2:16, 2:21-22, 3:3, 3:19).

How did I miss the obvious—that Jesus was the main proponent of folks needing to repent? Well, first of all, sin blinds (which may explain why I could read the gospels again and again and not see what was clearly written on the pages). But perhaps another reason a 'repentance preaching Jesus' wasn't on my radar screen was because that kind of message didn't fit with who I needed Him to be. I needed a nice Jesus who loved me and wanted above all else for me to be happy. I needed an affirming, non-judgmental Savior who would be tolerant rather than condemning. Being told I had to repent would have felt like a big guilt trip and I certainly didn't need that dumped on me. Eventually, as I plunged deeper into sin, becoming all the more deceived, thoughts of needing to repent all but vanished. During brief moments of minimal spiritual consciousness when I sensed all was not quite right in my life, (usually after a relationship ended) any thought of repenting was quickly snuffed out by a decision to find another partner (as quickly as possible) and make it work. It wasn't until relationship #12 blew up in my face that I decided the new low to which I had sunk was as low as I wanted to go! That was it. I got down on my knees and prayed, *God, you're right, I'm wrong. You've been right all along. I'm done.* Simple and to the point. I wasn't sobbing nor in sackcloth with ashes smeared all over my face. My confession lacked the depth and elegance expressed by David in the fifty-first Psalm, but it was every bit as sincere and genuine.

The Greek word in the New Testament for repent is ***metanoea.*** It means that there is a transformative change of one's heart. In other words, the inner self is changed resulting in spiritual conversion. But it also means a transformation of the mind. Simply put, it means to think differently. Although I had been living in rebellion and disobedience to the word of God, I tend to believe I was in a backslidden state rather than an unregenerate sinner, as I had given my life to Christ when I was ten. There are those who will disagree, arguing there's no way an active homosexual can be a child of God. Perhaps they are right but I'm going to sidestep that debate focusing rather on the change that began to take place in my mind once I turned away from sin and bolted toward the Savior. And believe me, after decades of distorted thinking, this would be no small undertaking!

In the weeks and months that followed, I found myself abhorring the sin of homosexuality. Often, when a life has been ravished by sinful choices, the tendency is just to abhor the consequences the wayward behavior produced. I admit, that was more than likely the main motivator that brought me to my knees that September morning. While it was an acceptable place to start—as the dire consequences I had brought on myself left me broken enough for God to get my attention—it was not the place I was meant to stay. Fortunately, as I matured in Christ, my abhorrence of sin stemmed out of love and devotion to Jesus because I saw how my transgressions offended His holiness and grieved His heart. When I truly began to comprehend it was my iniquities that put Him on a cross, I came to loathe my homosexual past—every last part of it.

As I travelled further away from my sinful past and regained some spiritual sanity, it became abundantly clear that repentance had been the doorway into all the wonderful benefits purchased for me by Jesus at Calvary. When the Holy Spirit shed light into my darkness, and my mind experienced renewal, I did an about face. I ran away from iniquity and straight towards God—finding in His heart a storehouse of divine treasure. Repentance was the starting point. Apart from repenting, there would have been no deliverance from the power of sin, no healing of heart wounds, no mind renewal and no capability to love in a healthy, Christ honoring way. Little did I realize that all these awesome perks awaited me once I confessed my sin, admitted God was right and allowed my mind to be transformed by Scripture. All I was hoping for was that I'd be given the strength to stop acting out sexually and be kept from ever getting into another relationship.

It would take some time before I understood that the Lord's desire for my life was total liberation from emotional attraction to women and complete healing of all the wounds fueling those attractions. The focus in the early days after repenting was behavior modification. My goal was simply to not wander off into sin again. A friend suggested it would help to find a support group with others who had repented of homosexual sin. That sounded like a great idea and so I sought out such a group. Unfortunately, I came up empty. At the time I was disappointed, but it actually turned out to be a blessing. The group I was trying to hook up with firmly believed homosexual attraction was a permanent gig—something most live with for the rest of their lives (which is what 99% of the Christians I converse with also believe). Being protected from hearing this bleak prognosis allowed my heart to remain open and receptive to what was coming down the pike. Lo and behold, it turned out to be way beyond anything I could have imagined—"infinitely beyond my highest prayers, desires, thoughts or hopes" (Eph. 3:20b LB).

Chapter 4

CHANGING MY MIND

A few months into my new life in Christ I sensed the Holy
Spirit prompting me to do specific things. It began with
the decision to have my home become a television free zone.
It wasn't so much because I was watching anything vile and
disgusting, because I wasn't. Granted, finding shows that
didn't flaunt immorality or plaster too much violence all over
the screen greatly limited my choices. However, I did manage
to get hooked on a couple programs such as, Ghost Whisperer
and Without a Trace. But what pushed me over the edge were
all the stupid commercials bombarding my sensibilities night
after night. Every last one of them was out to convince me of
some serious lack in my life and if I didn't run right out and
purchase whatever was being peddled, well I was just a total
loser. I was particularly bewildered by all the advertisements
from drug companies, touting pills that addressed every single
ailment known to mankind. These drugs were presented as
miracle cures—restoring one's life to the health and vitality

experienced back in grammar school. But then of course came the list of side-effects, many which could literally kill you. Think I'm kidding? If only. One commercial in particular, shown night after night advertised a wonderful new drug that helped those suffering from depression. One of the side-effects was suicide! (What's wrong with this picture?) I couldn't take it anymore. Soon thereafter it was, "Goodbye TV!"

With the televisions out of the house, I turned to viewing movies on my laptop as a source of entertainment. Through the years I had accumulated quite the collection of DVDs and in no time flat I was having a good old time watching them. But before long, my fun was disrupted when once again I felt a nudging in my spirit that I needed to purge my library. Seeing how all the movies I owned were, drama/romance 'chick-flicks' the litmus test for a DVD remaining in my collection was simply this: was there fornication in the movie? In saying that perhaps you're assuming I had some pretty sleazy flicks on my shelves. But that was not the case. West Side Story, Somewhere in Time, The Notebook, In Harm's Way, Top Gun, Pretty Woman, (just to name a few) were PG rated at worst. Unmarried couples being sexually intimate had become so commonplace in movies that I hardly gave it a second thought. And to be perfectly honest—it didn't offend me. Looking back, I realize that sin is easily camouflaged when committed by gorgeous people, while beautiful music plays in the background. And although there wasn't a single movie glorifying homosexuality in my home, I was starting to make a connection between that and fornication. As I became acclimated to premarital sex being the norm, homosexual relating became less of a big deal. In other words, one sin paved the way for the next one coming down the pike. So, if I was going to remain free and have any hope of my soul being restored, it was imperative to cut off anything and everything that put forth the toxic message that 'sin was no big deal'. All of that is to say, my stack of DVDs shrunk considerably.

Lastly, it was time to deal with the music my mind and spirit were ingesting. (*Ugh!*) I am a singer and one of my great joys in life is listening to other vocalists who are really, really good. I was in my thirties when CD players hit the market. One of my former partners bought me one for Christmas. Of course, they were humongous (weighing about fifty pounds), but I thought I had died and gone to heaven. Every payday I went to the local music store and bought as many CDs as my meager budget could afford. Well, by the time I reached my mid-fifties I had shelves full of glorious recordings. Every singer that gave me a thrill was right there at my fingertips. All I had to do was pop in a CD. Day and night, I was serenaded by Barbra Streisand, Natalie Cole, James Ingram, Whitney Houston, Julie Andrews, Al Jarreau and a host of other super stars. In my collection was a CD of Dionne Warwick singing Cole Porter tunes. I had been crazy about Dionne since my teens, and Cole Porter had become one of my favorite songwriters. I listened to that CD endlessly. But unfortunately, it had to go (with a whole host of others that I cherished).

If listening to a CD brought back thoughts and kicked up emotions from my not-so-gay days—it was, "Adios." As I had done major daydreaming about being loved by the perfect woman while blasting this music in my car and home, the effect many of these CDs had on me was sort of like Pavlov's dog hearing the bell and starting to drool. For years I had trained my mind to flip over to the dark side the minute these songs hit the airwaves. Once I became aware of this connection, I knew what I had to do. The television leaving my life was relatively painless. It was a bit more difficult to part with some of my movies. But getting rid of the music I loved was really tough. And yet the desire of my heart was to be far, far away from my past life—both physically and emotionally. So, I did what I needed to do without whining or bellyaching. (Okay, maybe just a little whimpering.)

What the Lord was doing in having me rid these things from my life was cutting off the stimuli that triggered homosexual desires within me. Even though I was saturating my soul with the Word of God and listening to sermons and gospel CDs, taking in even a small amount of the old stuff would prevent a complete release from my sinful past. It would take several years before I understood the profound impact my thought life had on my entire being—body, soul and spirit. I knew there was a strong connection between thoughts and emotions, but I had no idea that the thoughts endlessly playing in my mind were causing physiological changes in my brain. But, one night, while Googling some things on the Internet, I ran across a very interesting and informative article explaining how repetitive thoughts affect the brain. I quickly came to realize what the movies and music I had been feasting on for years had done to my brain. The homosexual daydreams that formulated in my mind while listening to love songs and watching romance movies aided in the formation of what's known as a neural pathway. Science has never been my forte, but if I understand this correctly, having a thought activates neurons that send an electrical message to an axon which then gets routed to a connecting dendrite, causing a chemical messenger to stimulate more neurons. Thus, a neural pathway is formed.

I know, I know—what I just wrote made absolutely no sense but this is important information to grasp so perhaps an illustration will help. The house I grew up in was located a few blocks from a creek that led directly to our grade school. A lot of the kids in my neighborhood walked along that creek to and from school every day. Although it was the quickest route, it wasn't always the safest as we deemed it great fun to push each other into the muddy water. (For some reason my mother never saw the humor in it.) Over the years, that path had been travelled so frequently that what once was grass had become hard packed dirt—making it much easier to navigate and run away from evil classmates who were on a mission to knock their fellow school chums into the muck. ("Honest, Mom—it wasn't my fault!") This is kind of what happens to our brain when we think the same thought over and over again. We

29

actually forge what can be detected as a groove on the surface of our brain, thus allowing those repetitive thoughts traveling on it to become second nature and seemingly involuntary. Developing new thoughts requires a lot of work because you have to chart out new pathways. Those of us who are sixty and older can remember what it was like, being the first one to walk to school the morning after a fourteen-inch snow fall. (Back then there was no such thing as 'snow days'.) I have vivid memories of being sent to school in my size three boots, trudging along at a snail's pace with snow up to my thighs! Anyway, developing a new thought can be like that. At first it seems like an unattainable goal—establishing healthy thoughts after you've spent a lifetime cruising the dirt path alongside the creek. But in time, with persistence, discipline and a whole lot of God's grace, it will happen.

The compulsive thoughts that paved my pathway into homosexual desire began in the most innocent way. When I was nine years old, my father took me to see The Sound of Music. At that time my parents were going through a bitter divorce. In the sixties, most mothers were granted full custody of the children which meant I only saw Dad for an hour during the week and on Sunday afternoon. As my father was the love of my life I found this arrangement most distressing. Though my mom was in many ways a good parent, her struggles with depression and alcoholism hampered her ability to engage with her daughters on an emotional level. Needless to say, by age nine I was very needy—missing Dad and starving for Mom's love and affection. If you've ever seen The Sound of Music you can only imagine the powerful impact it had on my life. For those of you who have been living on Mars for the past fifty years, The Sound of Music is about a retired sea captain from the Austrian navy. Captain Von Trapp is a widower with seven children whom he treats like sailors aboard one of his ships. Into their lives comes a new nanny (Julie Andrews) who wants to become a nun but is continually causing a ruckus over at the convent. She is shipped off to take care of these love-starved kids while 'the powers that be' try to figure out if being a sister is really the gig for her. Lo and behold, she brings joy and laughter back into their hearts, she and the Captain fall in love, get married and they all live happily ever after. That's the gist of the movie and although the specifics of my life differed from that of the Von Trapp children, I could certainly identify when it came to being a love-starved child, in need of someone to lift me out of the sorrow I was drowning in. For the two plus hours I spent watching that movie, I was truly happy. My heart had so identified with their story, it was as if I had become part of that family.

When my nephew Scott was a little boy, he would cry at the end of movies that he liked. Right there in the middle of the theater he'd have a total melt down sobbing, "I don't want it to be over!" That's pretty much how I felt that afternoon and although I refrained from losing it, my face must have shown utter dismay as I was once again thrust back into my own sad reality. My father must have sensed how disappointed I was because he took me over to the souvenir table and bought me a present—the best gift I ever received from him. Dad purchased the soundtrack to the movie and lovingly placed it in my hands.

For the next many months I could be found next to our HiFi, in a red rocking chair listening to that record and staring at the picture of Julie Andrews on the back of the album jacket. As I rocked back and forth I would daydream about being one of the Von Trapp children with Julie as my wonderful, nurturing, loving mother who made me clothes out of curtains and sang songs to me all day. Between the motion of the rocking chair, the glorious music and the visual of Julie, I was able to attain a state of euphoria—thus escaping my sad and pathetic life for a brief period of time. My mother probably should have suspected something was amiss as what normal kid rocks in a chair all day listening to the same record again and again and again. But she wasn't about to ruin a good thing as I was entertaining myself and not getting on her nerves.

A few years later when I was in my early teens I was once again captivated by another Julie Andrew's movie called The Americanization of Emily. This 1964 film was a steamy romantic comedy in which she falls in love with James Garner, an American Naval officer stationed in London during World War 2. (What's with Julie and all these sailors?) Mind you, I already have an obsession firmly intact with Julie as a mother figure but after seeing this movie, it metastasized into Julie being the love of my life. The transition was effortless as for years I had been forging out a neural pathway named, 'Strolling Down Fantasy Lane with Julie'. I am convinced that my homosexual tendencies were conceived in that red rocking chair listening to The Sound of Music and birthed the night I saw The Americanization of Emily.

Only after repenting of my sinful past and doing some intensive inner healing work was I in a place to receive the truth concerning the root causes that had led me down a homosexual trail. After the Julie Andrews factor came to light, I remember feeling hurt, sad and rather outraged. How wrong and downright rude of Satan to go after a broken little nine-year old, innocently rocking in a red chair, listening to a beautiful Rogers and Hammerstein musical, just trying to find a little happiness amidst all her sadness. What right did he have to swoop in and corrupt such a precious moment? Surely there are rules even he has to abide by! How dare he! But then I recalled to mind words spoken by our Lord that identify the devil as the total creep he really is. "The thief comes only to steal and kill and destroy" (John 10:10a ESV). Very true and oh, so very sad. Still—I think there should be age restrictions as to who he can pick on and go after. But obviously there are not. Millions of abortions have made that painfully obvious.

Scripture makes no mention of neural pathways or the neurons, dendrites and axons that create grooves in our brain.

But it's a given that God knows all about these things seeing how He created every part of us and designed our complex operating system. Rather than providing the intricate details of our anatomy, the Bible cuts right to the chase. "Do not be conformed to this world, but be transformed by the renewal of your mind" (Romans 12:2a ESV). God obviously knew how our sin nature would mess up our minds and that every one of us would need to forge out some new pathways! Next, the Bible tells us how to do it. "Finally, brothers, whatever is true, whatever is honorable, whatever is just, whatever is pure, whatever is lovely, whatever is commendable, if there is any excellence, if there is anything worthy of praise, think about these things" (Philippians 4:8 ESV).

Once all of this came to light, I understood that to genuinely repent involved much more than a moment in time where I got down on my knees and completely owned that I had blown it, messed up, violated God's commandments and greatly grieved His heart. While forgiveness and reconciliation with the Father were instantaneous, changing my mind took time and it took effort. Until new pathways were formed, and healthy patterns of thinking became second nature, part of me would stay connected to my homosexual past. And although I had heard again and again by Bible-believing Christians that only the act was sinful and not the desire, I still wanted to be released from all of it. Turns out God wanted the same thing for me which is why He had the Holy Spirit prompt me to begin the purging process.

It all began with repenting. Having to humble my heart, own my stuff, walk away from all that was familiar and discard many things I was attached to was difficult and at times downright painful. But what followed was way more wonderful than anything I experienced on my most awful day during that purging process. I came to realize I was simply letting go of some rubbish "...in order that I might gain Christ" (Phil. 3:8 ESV).

Chapter 5

UNBOUND

A great part of my healing and deliverance from homosexual bondage came via the folks in the Catholic Charismatic Renewal. I will tell of my conversion to Catholicism and my decision to revert later, but it is important for me to say that some of the best friends I have ever had are Roman Catholics. Without their love and support, God only knows where I'd be. One such Catholic angel is my friend, Dr. Joan Darcy. I met Joan in the spring of 2010. I had just come into the Church and was less than a year out of homosexual relating. She was giving a lecture at the seminary where she taught, and it was my privilege to attend. The minute she finished speaking I made a mad dash to be the first one to speak to her. My initial greeting went something like this: "Hi, I'm Robin. I just became Catholic. I spent 35 years prior to this as an active homosexual and I am still kind of messed up. I need help!"

I suppose I should clarify what I meant by, 'messed up'. Simply this; I was behaving correctly and had absolutely no desire to go back into the muck and mire, but I knew that after decades of habitual sin, my inner self needed some major renovating. Dr. Darcy listened intently then responded by telling me that wasn't her area of expertise and suggested her colleague, Dr. Jans would be better equipped to help me. *Yes, Yes,* I thought to myself. *I'm sure Dr. Jans is terrific but right now she's nowhere to be found and I seriously need some help!*

Out of desperation I mustered up the courage to ask Joan for her email address, which she graciously provided. Soon thereafter I began sending her emails and was pleasantly surprised with the promptness in which she answered every single one of them. In the weeks that followed she graciously took me under her wing and began aiding me along the road to recovery. One day I received a book from her called, <u>Prison to Praise</u>. It was based on the premise that as we praise the Lord in all things (1 Thessalonians 5:17) the power of the Holy Spirit is unleashed in our lives. While I was touched by her thoughtful gesture, what made that gift from Joan even more special is that I had read this book years earlier, before I wandered off into the abyss. It was as if God was saying, "Let's begin again."

Several weeks later, Joan and I met at the Catholic Church she attended to celebrate the Pentecost Vigil Mass. The plan was for her to pray a fresh outpouring of the Holy Spirit on me. God, who is ever faithful, kind and gracious, answered her prayer that night. Oh, how He loves when His children want more of Him. But the Lord God is also omniscient and knowing what was in store for me, He saw fit to rekindle my spirit—thus preparing me for what was coming down the pike.

It wasn't long after the Pentecostal Vigil that Joan sent me an email saying she knew of some folks who were willing to pray for me and asked if I would be open to that. Being a fervent believer in the power of prayer, I responded with an enthusiastic, "Yes!" So, Joan gave my contact information to an individual affiliated with a ministry called Unbound. Before they would meet with me I was required to read the book by Neal Lozano (Unbound) in order to understand the process and know what I was signing up for. My friends Ed and Donna caught wind of these plans and as a gesture of support bought the book for me (which really touched my heart). Once that book was in my hands I read it as quickly as possible figuring the sooner they prayed for me, the better. Unfortunately, this wasn't the kind of book conducive for speed reading, so I really didn't comprehend much of what was on the pages. (Thank God there was no quiz to take or I'd have been sent right back home!) The long and short of it? I walked into that session quite clueless as to what was about to take place. Yet at the same time I was confident something good was going to happen, otherwise Joan would have never suggested it.

My session was held on a Saturday afternoon in June of 2010. It was an absolutely beautiful day—the kind of day one spends out on the golf course or riding their bike down a country road (not cooped up in a car, driving across town to go sit inside some building). Although I was still grateful to have people willing to help me get well, I was slightly bummed it had to happen on the perfect day to work on my tan. (I wish I were kidding but this is how self-obsessed I was.) But upon arriving my spirit suddenly perked up as I noticed people sitting outside and soaking up glorious rays of sunshine as they prayed. (*Hallelujah! Where's the Coppertone?*) My joyful disposition, however, was short lived when the prayer team I was assigned to asked if I was okay with praying indoors as they were hot from sitting in the sun. I smiled and told them that would be fine. (Okay—so right off the bat I lied, but it seemed less sinful than pitching a hissy fit over the foiling of my plans.)

The Unbound prayer process is quite specific and rather involved. Neal Lozano takes 239 pages to explain it and the fact that I'm about to spell it out in a single paragraph could very well land me in his doghouse. But seeing how highly unlikely it is he'll be one of the ten people who will actually read this book, I'm probably in the clear so here goes.

Most of us who are wounded have folks from our past and from the present moment as well, that we have not forgiven for things they did to us. Unforgiveness always morphs into something harmful to the soul such as bitterness, resentment, self-pity and perhaps even hatred. These emotions become impediments to our freedom in Christ and hinder our ability to heal. I kind of visualize these toxic feelings as balls and chains that many of us lug around day in and day out. The

Unbound process walks a person back in time, guiding them through a specific process which helps them forgive those they harbor ill will towards—resulting in liberation from spiritual captivity. The sessions last 90 minutes and a ministry team of two meets with each individual. One person sits quietly off to the side and does intercessory prayer. The other member of the ministry team is the spiritual tour guide who takes you back to dark memories from days gone by that you really don't want to revisit (at least I didn't) and coaches you through the forgiveness process. This is the basic gist of what Unbound seeks to accomplish. Those wanting more details should read the book but for my purposes in writing this chapter, this is sufficient information.

I had a lot of people to deal with during those 90 minutes. The list was seemingly endless of folks who had gotten on my nerves, ticked me off and just plain done me wrong. For starters, there were my parents. I could have spent the entire session on them alone. There were teachers who had hurt me (going all the way back to grade school), former ministers, ex-partners (all twelve of them), my siblings, school chums, neighborhood kids and some fellow church members. On some level I knew that most of them never meant to hurt me. Truth be told, I was a very needy, high maintenance child and could be totally overwhelming. I was forever getting in other people's space and when they gently backed me off because they needed some breathing room, I took it as rejection (which left me feeling hurt and wounded). So, the list was long and I probably could have filled half an arena with all the folks I felt harmed by. But interestingly, the person I was by far the most angry with was myself. Not only had I completely messed up my own life, I had wreaked havoc in the lives of countless others along the way by being selfish and acting wickedly. The guilt and shame I bore over the hurt I inflicted on the people in my life was massive! With this being my story, it was going to be, 'Mission Impossible' to mention every person by name during that ninety-minute session. There were just too many people. But God, ever rich in mercy, was undeterred from accomplishing His good work in me that afternoon, regardless if some names weren't spoken out loud. He, who doeth all things well, showed up in a great big way and showered on me a triple dose of His love! Here's what happened.

For over an hour, I named one person after another who had wounded my heart, freely offering forgiveness to each of them. As time began to expire and it became apparent there was still a lot of territory to cover, my prayer guide began to lump some folks together—namely, my former partners. Looking back, I probably needed an Unbound weekend retreat, but nonetheless, God, seeing the sincerity of my heart and already knowing the names of each and every person that hadn't been audibly spoken by me, swept my heart clean—ridding it of all bitterness, resentment and hurt. The reason I know this to be the case is because at the end of my session a bolt of joy went right into the center of my heart. I kid you not! The grief and sadness I had lived with for years was immediately replaced with a sensation of total bliss. It may sound like I'm being overly dramatic in describing what I felt but I'm telling the truth. I had never felt anything like that before and I haven't since. (*Bummer.*)

When the session had ended, I got up out of my chair (smiling from ear to ear), said my goodbyes and started walking to the car. Within moments I became aware of a very strange sensation. It felt like I was walking on air. Really and truly it did! "Oh Lord, this is so fun!" I said while laughing aloud. How totally bizarre. Had I lost a hundred pounds during that ninety-minute session or had the earth's gravity suddenly relaxed a bit? I was so hoping the 'Moon Walk' sensation would hang with me for a while, but it didn't. By the time I got home my feet were firmly back on the planet. The best I can figure is that God allowed me to have that experience, if only for a brief time, to let me know that the balls and chains that had weighed me down for decades had indeed fallen off.

There was one more gift (#3 if you're counting) that the Lord gave me via Unbound and unlike the sensation of walking on air, this one has been permanent. But in order to understand the magnitude of its significance, we need to go on a slight detour, taking a step back in time.

As previously revealed, my dad was the love of my life. He left us during the summer of 1963, a couple months shy of my 8th birthday, right before I entered the 3rd grade. One of the tragic outcomes resulting from his departure was the near-fatal hit my heart suffered when it came to having feelings toward the opposite sex—resulting from a fear of abandonment. The shutting down of emotions concerning every male on the planet was more than likely an attempt at self-preservation. While there were a couple of boyfriends along the way, there were no sparks flying on my part. I felt a little excitement that I had a boyfriend but the guy himself usually bored me. However, in the ninth grade I felt some affection towards one of my teachers. He wasn't particularly handsome and was more of a father figure rather than someone I wanted to go steady with. Nonetheless, God used this man to start softening up my heart. Shortly thereafter, another man would enter my life and he would be the one to arouse in me all the love and adoration I felt as a child.

In the fall of 1970 I began high school. Loving to sing and being somewhat good at it, I signed up for the girl's glee club. As incoming sophomores, our initiation was to get up as a group and sing the school fight song. Basically, all we had to do was get most of the melody right and not mess up the words too much. That morning I showed up with my ukulele and told our accompanist, Mrs. M, she could sit this one out. To put a little icing on the cake I harmonized as I strummed along. While my classmates undoubtedly thought I was an obnoxious showoff, (which I was), our choir director, Mr. Calvin, was completely smitten. That was the beginning of a very affectionate relationship which evolved between us.

His wife, who happened to be a school employee as well, was also part of this lovefest. While I adored them both, I was absolutely crazy about Mr. C. He became the father figure I so desperately needed.

The Calvins had three sons and began to refer to me as 'the daughter they never had'. (They were without a doubt the parents I always wanted!) Knowing that I was from a poor home, Mrs. Calvin hired me to help her clean her house on occasion. Sometimes I would get to spend the night and ride to school with them the next morning. The summer before I went to college, I was invited to vacation with them at their cottage in Northern Michigan. By today's standards, one might jump to the conclusion that some boundaries were crossed. But things were much more relaxed in the early 1970s. When a teacher encountered a needy student such as I, there was more freedom to take them into your heart and home. I am convinced that their every act of kindness was well intentioned and that they genuinely cared about me.

For three straight years I began each school day camped outside the choir room door, anxiously waiting for the Calvins to arrive. Weekends were depressing, and summers were awful as I missed the everydayness of our relationship. I was very dependent on them and my intense neediness was an indication that my emotional maturity hadn't evolved much since age seven when Dad departed. As graduation approached I began to internally lose it. I was seriously on the verge of falling apart in anticipation of being abandoned once again.

My heart's desire was to remain in high school the rest of my life as I couldn't imagine my life without them! Only by the grace of God did I make it through graduation without the aid of medication or worse yet, being locked up in a psych ward.

A few days after receiving my diploma there I was, back in the choir room hanging out with Mr. C, helping him tidy things up before he closed up shop for the summer (and sent me off into an abyss of gloom and despair). Perhaps he sensed how sad I was. I never expressed my feelings to him, but it was probably written all over my face that I was dying inside. Mr. Calvin was sitting at the table where he did much of his work and I was standing right next to him. Out of the blue he looked me right in the eyes and spoke these words. "Now that you've graduated, we don't have to hide how much we love you."

My heart melted inside of me. (*Really? Can I have that in writing?*)

It was the best and most wonderful thing anyone had ever said to me in my entire life. And upon hearing those words the dark cloud that was hanging over me was instantly dissolved. I don't remember saying anything out loud but inwardly I was jumping for joy and shouting, *YAHOO!!!* From that moment on I had the assurance it was safe to go off to college and enjoy the next phase of my journey. I felt absolutely confident that my adopted parents were always going to love me and be an integral part of my life. It meant everything to know I would forever be their daughter.

So off to college I went and when I came home on weekends, my first call was to the Calvins as I couldn't wait to see them. But right from the start, things were different. Phone calls lasted no more than five minutes (if that) and rarely did they invite me over.

What's up? Why are they treating me like this? I thought we were family, I asked myself, again and again.

Because I was such a deeply wounded individual, my perception of reality and ability to interpret the motives of others accurately was often skewed. That being the case, I concluded that I really wasn't their daughter—just a former student who sang well, absorbed everything I was taught like a little sponge, and for a moment in time was the star pupil. In hindsight, they were probably just letting go so I could get on with my life. But I felt like I had been replaced by other kids and no longer mattered to them.

Ironically, I didn't cry… didn't get angry…didn't fall apart or talk to anyone about what had happened. Looking back, I wish I had done all of the above. Perhaps then I could have gotten some much needed help. But instead, I just died inside. Losing another dad was more than I could bear. I was unable to survive being abandoned for a second time by a father figure I trusted and loved. As a result, my heart went completely numb when it came to men. My ability to feel any affection or emotional love for a member of the opposite sex was zero. I didn't hate guys, they just didn't spark my heart in any way, shape or form. As far as men went, my heart had flatlined!

This is the condition I was in when I showed up for my Unbound session. There were several ministry teams present the day I was scheduled to be prayed with and I had no idea who I'd be assigned to. I would have preferred a female prayer duo, but God had other plans. The team I was paired up with was mixed—one man and one woman. Though disappointed, I wasn't devastated (although I did feel a little apprehensive when the female member of this team immediately trotted off to a corner to begin her role as intercessor). That left me all alone and face-to-face with my male tour guide whose name was John. He seemed like a nice enough guy and, again, it wasn't as if I hated men that made me feel a tad uneasy—I just couldn't let them within a mile of my heart. So as long as he kept his distance, stayed on his side of my protective wall and I wasn't expected to emotionally bond with him, then we'd get along just fine.

John began by situating his chair directly in front of mine (so close our kneecaps were almost touching). Strangely, I found that to be comforting rather than anxiety provoking. During the next hour and a half, as I divulged one dark secret after another, John would often reach out and touch my arm, attempting to soothe me when he sensed a painful memory had surfaced. The things I shared that afternoon were vile, sinful and just downright ugly—yet there I was, allowing a total stranger (a man, no less) to have access to that horrific mess! Amazingly, John never once became judgmental. He didn't make horrible faces or respond with, "YOU CAN'T

BE SERIOUS!" when he learned I had twelve relationships and that we needed to revisit every single one of them. I found him to be gentle, kind and most of all, loving. As he allowed the Holy Spirit to flow through him, ministering to my wounded soul, something miraculous happened. God put a crack in the wall surrounding my heart. I wasn't aware that I was missing a brick or two when the session had concluded, I just knew that John was a sweetie and I really liked that we sat knee cap to knee cap, so he could reach out and touch me a bunch of times. It was in the weeks to come that I noticed a strange phenomenon taking place. My heart was once again responding to men. Since 1973 no man had been able to evoke the slightest signal on the monitor; there was nothing but a continual flat line running across the screen. But, at some point during the 90-minute session, a bleep appeared, and then another and another... God used John—a kind, sensitive, compassionate man to resurrect my emotionally unresponsive heart and bring me back to life. In the months that followed I would start to trust, be vulnerable and reawaken to the reality that having guys close to my heart was actually quite wonderful.

My healing journey began with Unbound. This ministry was the first stop along the way on the road to recovery. It would have been difficult, if not impossible, to receive what Jesus had in store for me if still loaded down with fifty years of resentments, grudges and all the emotional baggage that comes with an unforgiving spirit. As I journeyed deeper into my wounded past, more hurtful memories accompanied by bitter feelings would surface. But I was able to use what I learned from John to keep on forgiving and releasing, knowing it would result in further healing and more freedom.

With this tool in my bag I was ready for what came next. Now mind you, I had no idea there even was a next step. I was completely clueless as to how one recovered from the fallout after decades of habitual sinning. And yet God knew there was a next stop along the restoration pathway, and He knew exactly what it was. He also appointed just the right person to make sure I'd get there. I wish I could tell you I was gently guided there in the same way I had been led to Unbound. But that was not the case. This time I wasn't given a voice in the matter—I was ordered to go! Needless to say, I wasn't one bit happy about it.

Chapter 6

SHEPHERD'S GROUP

I met Mary Ellen at a Catholic church near my house where both of us attended weekday liturgy. One morning after Mass we struck up a conversation. I was giving her my undivided attention until Fr. Socorro walked over. My focus immediately shifted to him, thus blowing off Mary Ellen in mid-sentence. As I walked home, I realized how poorly I had behaved and promptly asked the Lord to forgive me for being so rude. My self-imposed penance was to write Mary Ellen a letter, apologizing for my bad manners and seek her forgiveness. For good measure I included some pertinent information about myself as old people like that sort of thing. (Mary Ellen was in her early eighties when we met.) I think I told her how old I was, my dog's name and something else of great importance— like what my favorite cookie was. (It's chocolate chip.) Well, she was thrilled to have the inside scoop on me and from that moment on we were the best of friends.

I had no plans to tell Mary Ellen about my horrible past, after all, why did she need to know that? Wasn't it enough she knew my age and favorite cookie? What if this news caused her to have a heart attack or stroke? Then what? No— this information would be withheld for the sake of Mary Ellen's health. But one night I realized I needed to tell her. We were driving home from a charismatic prayer meeting we had attended, along with Antoinette, another woman from our parish. I was growing emotionally close to both of them and it was obvious they had affection for me. Fearing rejection if they ever found out, I had to make a decision. How much more of my heart was I going to invest if it was going to end up broken? I think I was also starting to feel deceitful—sharing much of my life story with them and then having to skate around the three and a half decades spent in a toxic swamp. (For example, "How come I never married?")

So, there we were that night, yours truly behind the wheel, barreling down the expressway at 65mph with all the doors locked. I figured it was a good time to spill the beans as they'd be less likely to jump out the door, giving me a little time to talk them down if one or both of them started to come unglued. Well, thanks be to God no one fainted, needed CPR or attempted to dive out the window. Actually, they were both wonderful—responding with compassion, mercy and love. For that I was immensely grateful. But shortly thereafter I began to have second thoughts about how wise it had been on my part to let Mary Ellen know where I had come from. Allow me to explain.

One night, Mary Ellen phoned to let me know there was an inner healing group starting up at the Catholic Church next door to my apartment complex. (I had recently moved out of walking range to the parish we met at for weekday Mass.) Since she now was privy to my messed-up past, she was adamant that I needed to be part of this group! She promptly gave me the number of the woman in charge and instructed me to call her (with the same urgency a mother tells their ten-year-old to grab his coat and make a run for the school bus which just went barreling past the house). Before she let me go she nonchalantly slipped in that the group would be meeting on Saturday mornings at 8 a.m.—to which I rolled my eyes and immediately decided this wasn't the group for me. As soon as I hung up, I tossed Ann's number (the group leader) on my kitchen counter and ignored it for the next two weeks at which time I received yet another phone call from Mary Ellen.

"Have you called Ann?" she wanted to know.

Of course I haven't called her. That stupid group meets at 8 a.m. on Saturday mornings! That was the crux of the matter but instead I replied, "No, Mary Ellen, I haven't gotten around to it."

I was hoping that fib would buy me a little more time to come up with an acceptable excuse as to why I couldn't be part of this group. Instead, I heard a huge sigh coming through the phone receiver—the kind you hear when you've exasperated someone and are pretty sure they're entertaining thoughts of choking you.

"Okay, fine," she huffed. "I'll call her."

She immediately hung up on me. (*Whatever!*) Five minutes later my phone rang again and it's you know who. She was calling this time to inform me that Ann would be expecting me in the morning for the 8 a.m. Saturday gathering from Purgatory! No discussion—no getting out of it—like it or not, I was going.

The next morning, I rolled out of bed, put on my exercise clothes, and without even bothering to comb my hair I dragged myself over to the inner healing meeting. (I did however brush my teeth.) The group was small (I think there were eight of us in attendance that first week). We met in the basement of a building where centuries earlier nuns had resided and sat on couches that were so uncomfortable not even St. Vincent DePaul would take them. Ann had us go around the room, introduce ourselves and share a little about what brought us to this group. I thought about blaming Mary Ellen when it was my turn but came up with a better plan. I told them my name and then got right down to business, unloading my horror story on them in 30 seconds flat.

"Hi, I'm Robin. I was in gay life for 35 years, had 12 relationships, attended dozens of churches, caused chaos and disruption in the life of every person who spent more than five minutes with me, and then one day when I finally figured out how totally messed up my life was, I repented and became Catholic. It was suggested by someone I'm currently mad at that I participate in this Saturday morning gathering to do whatever we are going to do here." (Okay—so maybe not my exact words but close enough.)

My plan was to get sent home and be told this might not be the group for me, thus returning to sleeping in on Saturday mornings. No such luck. The ladies didn't start screaming, "LORD HAVE MERCY!" No one ran out of the building and they didn't even pull out their rosaries and beg Mary to intercede for me! Ann calmly thanked me for sharing and said they were all glad I had come. (*Really? Don't you want to think about it for a couple weeks and call me with your verdict?*)

Well that was that. I was going to be part of the inner healing group even if they decided to change the time to 6 a.m. (Thank the Lord they never did.) Bottom line? I was stuck! (*Great.*) But after the first week or two my attitude changed. I soon realized that I needed this group and it wasn't very long before I was appreciative that Mary Ellen forced me into it (even though I kept that secret from her for a long while— fearing she'd find more weekend groups for me to join that met before the sun was up).

So, what did we do at Shepherd's Group? Well, we began with praise and worship. (*No, you can't be serious asking me to sing at 8 a.m.!*) When Ann started the songs, they were usually so low we sounded more like a gathering of frogs at the neighborhood pond. (Totally pathetic). After I suffered through our singing we did a lesson from a little book we purchased from Ann. Each week we had Scriptures to read and questions to answer. We were probably supposed to come prepared, doing our lesson at home but half the time I showed up not even having opened my book, which was how I always operated when it came to doing homework. (How I made it through high school let alone college is a total mystery.) In my defense, I knew we were going to read the chapter together and the questions were the kind I could answer on the spur of the moment because they dealt with things like broken relationships, painful emotions, childhood wounds and stuff like that. (I needed zero prep time when it came to talking about my issues and all the people I had them with.) We would each have a turn to share our answers and after that, we prayed for one another.

As we prayed, Ann encouraged us to listen to the Holy Spirit and be open if He gave us a word of knowledge for the person we were praying for. Each of us brought a journal to Shepherd's Group and when it was our turn to be prayed over, one of the other gals took our journal and wrote down what words were spoken over us. When Ann dropped that little tidbit on us, I for one was ready to run out the door. Answering questions that dealt with my deepest pain and darkest secrets was a piece of cake. Hearing from Jesus? Not so much! When we prayed for each other on week one we all pretty much shrugged our shoulders and said, "I didn't get anything," (which was our way of saying, we hadn't heard squat). In those early sessions, I was usually giving a psychological analysis regarding what the gals had shared when answering the questions in our little books and passing it off as coming from Jesus. But in time we all began to get a sense of the Spirit's nudgings. And even though none of us could hear from the Lord like Ann did, each of us went home with a few more words of knowledge written in our journals as a result of being prayed over.

The goal of Shepherd's Group was to awaken our spirits to the reality that Jesus was indeed our good shepherd. "The Lord is my shepherd; I shall not want" (Psalm 23:1 KJV). Most of us can quote that entire Psalm in our sleep but few of us grasp the awesomeness of what it means to have the Lord as our shepherd. We have a shepherd that provides; (vs.1), a shepherd that leads; (vs.2), One who restores; (vs.3), anoints; (vs.5) and a shepherd that chases after us every day of our lives to douse us with His goodness and mercy; (vs.6). This is just skimming the surface of what it means to be part of His flock and under His care. In the New Testament, the Lord Jesus, our good shepherd, added another important component to the relationship between Himself and His sheep. "My sheep hear my voice, and I know them, and they follow me" (John 10:27 KJV). Perhaps that was why we were encouraged to listen for what He was saying as we prayed for each other on Saturday mornings. Our spiritual ears were being trained. I am so grateful that Ann stayed the course and didn't cave in when we all looked at her with panic-stricken eyes, as if she had just asked us to recite all of Leviticus from memory! Within time, most of us began to hear from the Spirit and started to speak His words of encouragement to one another.

When I walked away from my homosexual past I was well aware of the fact that I didn't know how to have wholesome relationships with women. So early in my recovery I began a quest to find some sort of list identifying all the DO's and DON'T's, regarding appropriate behavior with one's own gender. It needed to be spelled out for me—"This is acceptable; that is out of bounds. This is a normal thing we feel about each other; that feeling needs to be curtailed a bit." But that list was nowhere to be found. (*Oh come on. Someone must know where it is!*) Thankfully, God's plans for me were not hampered or contingent on my finding a manual of rules and regulations. While His goal was the same as mine, (forming healthy relationships with other gals), He knew a much better way to achieve that end.

One Saturday morning, after months of attending Shepherd's Group, I had the most amazing insight. During our time of sharing it suddenly dawned on me that I was sitting amongst my very best friends whom I loved from the bottom of my heart. Without even being aware of what was happening, I had entered into meaningful, intimate, Christ-centered relationships with several of the ladies and there wasn't a drop of 'weirdness' involved. I finally had friendships that met the deep needs of my heart. The best part of all was that over time these relationships with my sweet gal pals from Shepherd's Group evolved into something even more wonderful than friendships. I now had family. That's really what I had been seeking from partner after partner—only to end up disappointed and empty, time and time again. How very foolish I had been to not know that the God who loved me wanted that for me as well.

I could fill chapters documenting all the ways my wonderful friends from Shepherd's Group brought joy to my life with example after example of how they gave of their time, energy and treasure. Suffice it to say, I am grateful, grateful, grateful for their unconditional love. In spite of all my flaws and many sins such as self-centeredness, arrogance, endless complaining (just to name a few)—they never gave up on me. Instead, they remained true blue and loyal. (Although they probably wanted to drown me in holy water on more than one occasion).

Does every person coming out of homosexual bondage need to attend Shepherd's Group? My personal opinion is that it would be very beneficial. But I'm not sure how widespread this particular ministry is and if other churches around the country have ever even heard of it. With that being said, I strongly urge participation in a small group with the focus being on inner healing. Small groups cultivate intimacy among members and these relationships are hopefully centered on the Lord Jesus. Our group met regularly for eighteen months. That was a sufficient amount of time to do some intensive healing and form strong bonds of friendships. We met twice a month, but some folks may do better meeting weekly. There are no hard and fast rules as to how often to gather and how long to continue. The important thing is to just hook up with a group and allow the Lord to work in your life. There's only one thing I am adamant about. Make sure that your group is spending a significant amount of time praying for each other. Honestly, this really will bring about genuine love and closeness between members.

For those who are walking away (better yet, running) from homosexual sin, the small group setting is the best and safest place to develop God-centered relationships. Many Christians contend that reaching out to those who identify as homosexual, one to one, is the way to go. I concede that there are situations where this strategy has produced positive results. But be that as it may, I'm not totally convinced it is the wisest course of action. As societal norms have fallen by the wayside it has become increasingly difficult to maintain safe and healthy boundaries in relationships. Those of us sixty and older grew up with the understanding that our close and intimate friendships would be with those of our same gender and the 'love of our life' would be someone of the opposite sex. If a woman became best friends with a guy at church, the odds were pretty good that they were going to fall in love (since God created men and women to be attracted to one another). Everyone pretty much knew the rules for relating and understood that ignoring them could land you in murky waters. But it's a whole new ballgame and none of us are quite sure how the game is played. Not-so-gay men are attracted to and fall in love with other guys. So, if a brother at church decides to engage in a friendship with an avowed homosexual, there's a good chance the homosexual man will want more than that.

The same applies for women. Gals tend to connect more on an emotional level and in no time flat the relationship could become intense. That often opens the door for feelings to develop that cross the friendship line. Unfortunately, no matter how gentle and kind the rebuff, the already wounded person will feel hurt and rejected. They may very well conclude that Christians are the absolute worst people on the face of the earth and as far as they're concerned, someone needs to bring back the lions! Granted, there's always the possibility that with hard work, brutal honesty and the help of a professional counselor, it can be worked through. But if you want to play it safe and take a pass on your life turning into Days of Our Lives on steroids, just bring them into a small group setting. And if they are resistant to that, then find a ministry partner and reach out together. In New Testament times, more often than not, folks ministered in pairs. Jesus sent His guys out two by two (Mark 6:7). The Apostle Paul always had a ministry partner—first Barnabas (Acts 13:2) and later Silas (Acts 15:40). If you are in a healthy marriage, your best ministry partner will be your spouse. God can greatly use a solid marriage to aid those coming out of sexual bondage towards healing and wholeness. However, at the end of the day I still strongly encourage participation in a small group that is focused on inner healing.

I will forever cherish the fond recollections of those early Saturday morning gatherings, sitting on couches that caused back spasms and hyperventilating with my new friends as Ann kept telling us Jesus was speaking but none of us had a clue what He was saying! I have since sat among other small groups and will more than likely participate in a few more before my days on Earth are done. But thus far nothing has come close to the special bond of love I felt with my Shepherd's Group sisters and the internal healing we all experienced.

Feeling much better and having a relative amount of stability in my life, I stopped attending Shepherd's Group. As far as I was concerned, I was well enough. (*Nothing left to fix here!*) I had acquired some great friends, was faithfully attending church, consistently having quiet times and living each day totally free from homosexual desires. End of story—*I'm just fine* (so I thought). But Ann insisted there was more. As far as she was concerned, I needed to do some deeper healing than we had done at our Saturday morning group. (*Really?*) There would be no questions to answer in a workbook and I wasn't required to bring a journal. All that would be needed was a box of Kleenex and some extra strength Tylenol to deal with the headache I'd have after crying my eyes out. I was off to Theophostic!

Chapter 7

THEOPHOSTIC

If Ann said it once, she said it a thousand times, "You need to do Theophostic." It was usually after one of us had a major melt down at Shepherd's Group during prayer time or had unloaded some horrific memory from childhood during the sharing session, confessing how we still struggled with feelings of worthlessness as a result of what had happened to us! "Theophostic!" she would say, handing over a box of tissue. Everything was Theophostic. If I called her up to complain about my father she'd respond, "You need to do Theophostic, Robin." If my dog was on my last nerve and I called to crab about that I would hear, "Theophostic!" It got to the point that whatever I was dealing with in my life, the remedy always came back to my need for... you guessed it—THEOPHOSTIC!!! I got so sick of hearing about Theophostic I decided to do it just to shut her up.

Theophostic is a very strange word. Actually, it's a combination of two Greek words: *Theo* which means, God and *phostic* meaning, light. This prayer technique was developed by a therapist named Ed Smith. Theophostic turned out to be even more complicated and involved than what I had experienced in the Unbound prayer session. Those who feel called into this ministry must go through intensive training and not being trained myself, I am ill equipped to give an in-depth explanation of all the ins and outs that come into play during Theophostic prayer. But as I share my personal experience I think you'll get the gist of how it works and will hopefully be convinced it's a powerful ministry, worthy of further investigation.

Ed Smith discovered in working with clients who had suffered childhood trauma, that even more detrimental than the actual event was the lie they believed about themselves resulting from it. Making matters all the worse, the lie was often accompanied by a vow which was made in order to protect oneself from further injury. For example, there are countless cases in which sexually abused girls believed the lie that the abuse was their fault and vowed (be it conscious or unconscious) to keep men at a distance. Without healing, all this baggage is carried throughout the duration of one's life, making it nearly impossible to attain loving, intimate relationships. This scenario not only pertains to sexual abuse victims but also to a whole host of other childhood injuries where precious, vulnerable souls were seriously harmed. The list is varied and seemingly endless in the things that can gash open a child's heart but the outcome is often the same: a traumatic event gives birth to a lie, an ill-fated vow springs forth and the wounded person spends the rest of their life trying to figure out why their relationships aren't working. Fortunately, God shared with Ed Smith what could be done about it.

How does one decipher if they are in need of inner healing and are a candidate for Theophostic? Most of the time the best indicator for me is when I overreact to a situation. Someone once told me I was putting on a little weight. It was meant as a compliment, but I went home and exercised for six hours! This overreaction was fueled by an incident from childhood that was painful and downright cruel. Growing up I had a minister who told me on more than one occasion I was getting fat. That innocent comment about my putting on weight tapped directly into a fifty-year-old wound. (*Ouch!*) This is what's known as a trigger (of which I had many). One of my triggers that can still get flicked happens when folks are tardy. (Instant irritation.) This definitely takes me back to a scene from childhood that was repeated on a regular basis.

When my parents divorced, Mom was given full custody of us and Dad had visitation rights (one night during the week and every Sunday afternoon). My parents operated in different time zones. Mom arrived everywhere she went an hour early and Dad showed up at least an hour late. (That marriage was toast from the start.) If Dad was supposed to pick us up on Sunday at 1 p.m., our mother had us standing by the front door at noon, where we waited and waited and waited for dear old Dad to pull into the driveway. Once Dad hit the ten-minute tardy mark, Mom began ripping on him for once again being late. His tardiness was just the tip of the iceberg.

Mom had a list a mile long of things she found egregious and irritating about her former husband, so it was not at all difficult for her to fill our wait time with one derogatory remark after another about what a low life he was. Being very devoted and loyal to Dad, I rejected each and every one of her comments—instead believing his lateness was more about my unworthiness as his child, than some flaw in his character. *If I had any value at all, Dad would be on time*, I concluded.

The vow I made was that I would never be late, making someone have to wait on me. As a result, I arrive everywhere I go much too early (just like Mom) and if by chance I get stuck in traffic and it looks like I might be cutting it close—I immediately start panicking! (*Help me, Jesus!*) So, when church starts late because we're waiting for half the congregation who are still at McDonald's eating breakfast, those old thoughts resurface and I start feeling worthless— (*I'm not very impor-tant—my time doesn't matter…*) But instead of sinking into depression as I did during childhood, I now feel angry, which for me is the flip side of the coin. Years ago, my survival depended on protecting the hero status I bestowed upon Dad, so I took the anger out on myself. The annoying, late church attendees merit no such protection. I want to scream at every last one of them (which is why being a Sunday morning greeter is not my calling).

Although I had done psychotherapy during my 'anything-but-gay' days and had uncovered some of my past, I was still in much denial over how many of my triggers were being caused by historic events. I had spent a lifetime trying to forget huge chunks of childhood but in order to do Theophostic it was imperative to go back in time because all the lies I was believing had their origins there. Early in my recovery process, I was constantly denying that my five-hundred-dollar reaction to a five-dollar problem had anything whatsoever to do with yesteryear. Ann, however, was not dissuaded (no matter how many times I blew her off). She remained lovingly consistent, never changing her tune or giving me a pass— knowing very well that the majority of my unhappiness was rooted in childhood heartache.

As was the case with Unbound, Theophostic ministers work in teams of two. Ann's partner was a woman named Trisha. It was Trisha who sat first chair, conducting my Theophostic sessions. Ann's assignment was to be the inter-cessory prayer warrior. Ann had given me a heads up that Trisha was somewhat eccentric but assured me she was the best person to do Theophostic with because she could really hear from Jesus. Indeed, Ann was being straight with me. When God made Trisha, He threw out the mold! Like many saints of old, she was completely oblivious to the latest trends and not the least bit enslaved to the opinions of others. Trisha was so focused on pleasing the Lord she didn't have the time or energy to worry about impressing the rest of us. At first,

I was a bit intimidated and taken aback. Not only was she a no-nonsense sort of person but she was also extremely intense. There was no denying that Trisha was on a mission from God and her orders from on high were to help me get well. Having said all that, my apprehension was short-lived because I quickly discovered how kind, loving and compassionate she was and in no time flat my heart was completely set at ease.

My Theophostic sessions went something like this. We'd begin with me sharing a recent incident that caused me to short-circuit and lose my sanctification. Trisha would then ask, "What did you believe about yourself when that happened?" That was usually a difficult question to answer as my thoughts had been consumed with what a total moron the person who had ticked me off was. (If only she would have asked me what I believed about them!) But in Theophostic I had to deal with my own stuff (not the sins of others).

Once I had identified what I had believed about myself, Trisha asked a question that made me go back in time; "When was the first time you recall believing that about yourself?" If I replied, "College," Trisha would ask, "When before that?" "High school," I'd tell her hoping that would suffice her. But of course, it didn't. "Jr. high?" (I could tell by the look in her eyes that that wasn't the right answer either.) She never stopped pushing until we were at least back to grade school.

It was never easy getting to the origins of my damaged emotions as I had become a real pro when it came to burying pain and erasing hurtful events from my memory bank.

Because of that I wasn't always able to get all the way back to ground zero. But wherever I ended up, the next step was to recall the conclusive thought that was lodged into my mind and the vow that was made, as both had been affecting my emotional and mental well-being ever since.

Finally, Trisha would instruct me to take that thought to the Lord and ask Him one simple question; "Jesus, is that true?" Then I had to listen for what He had to say. The listening part for me was anxiety provoking. How could I be sure it was Jesus speaking? What if I was making it all up? I can't begin to tell you all the desperate looks I gave Ann when Trisha would ask me, "What is Jesus saying?" Ann was so much better at hearing from Him. I was so hoping she would slip me the answer, thus providing me with something to tell Trisha. But Theophostic doesn't work that way. Jesus needed to speak truth to the lie that was in **my** heart and it would only work if I heard from Him directly.

I don't remember much about my first session except I cried a lot, didn't remember much, and for the most part, was clueless as to what Jesus was saying to me. I went home with a whopping headache vowing my Theophostic days were over. Ann assured me that everyone felt awful after their first couple sessions but that it would get better so I should do it again soon. I don't know who was crazier—Ann for saying such a thing or me for believing her. Well, the long and short of it was, I went back for more torment, dug up other buried memories, exposed a multitude of lies and vows and, by the grace of God, began to hear from Jesus as He spoke the truth to my heart.

The specifics of my Theophostic sessions—historic events, lies believed, vows made and truths spoken by Jesus—were all written down by Ann and handed to me at the end of each session (pages upon pages). Unlike some folks who have newspapers in their homes from 1947, I throw everything out. (Once I tossed out my social security card. Oops!) So, Ann's meticulous records of all my sessions are long gone. I eventually convinced her to stop writing things down but here's what I remember. When I began my Theophostic journey I believed I was worthless and unworthy of love (especially where guys were concerned). One of the most detrimental myths that played over and over in my mind was that God had favorites and I wasn't one of them. Although I was probably misinterpreting Romans 9:13, "Jacob I loved, but Esau I hated," it often felt like I had been forgotten and forsaken by the God who was supposed to be in my corner. These lies were woven into the very fabric of my soul—manifesting themselves in all kinds of shapes and sizes. Trisha and Ann never seemed frustrated by having to deal with the same lies again and again because they both understood that their roots go deep and spread out in every direction. They remained patient but they were also relentless in pushing me back in time so I could locate the origins of these untruths.

One of the ways I hear from the Lord is through visual images and this was very much the case when I did

Theophostic. I had a vivid picture of meeting Jesus on top of a high mountain. As we sat together up there, I laid before Him the false beliefs I had been operating under for most of my life and then listened for Him to speak **truth** to my lies. In these visuals I saw myself as a small child, no more than six or seven years of age. Because the memories that came forth in Theophostic were often heart wrenching, I was continually sobbing my heart out during these face to face meetings with Jesus. In the midst of all this pain I envisioned His outstretched arms bidding me to come. I responded by running into His embrace and found there a closeness with God I had been longing for all my life. I'll go so far as to say it was in my Theophostic moments, up on that mountain top with Jesus, that I truly knew for the very first time how much God loved me.

While I'm not sure if this is part of everyone's Theophostic experience, I'm so glad it was part of my package deal. Perhaps it seems a bit bizarre that I saw myself high atop a mountain amidst puffy clouds, cuddling with Jesus. I get that for some this seems a bit over the top, unorthodox and perhaps even unbiblical—although I do recall reading somewhere that He carries His lambs in His bosom (Is. 40:11). But interestingly, several years after I had ceased doing Theophostic with Trisha and Ann, I came across a verse in the Psalms that made me smile. "Send out your light and your truth; let them guide me. Let them lead me to your holy mountain, to the place where you live" (Psalm 43:3 NLT). And, for the record—I have not since had the privilege of being up on that mountain top. I guess the Lord saw how wounded I was and knew that the only way I'd get well was to be brought up to His holy mountain where He could radiate me with His love.

According to Ed Smith, the goal of Theophostic is to learn to do it on your own because for those of us who have a multitude of wounds, there will always be triggers and more lies to root out. When this prayer technique becomes second nature, you can do it in the express lane at the grocery store when the shopper in front of you has 300 items in their basket! Instead of going off on them, have a Theophostic time out. If memory serves me correctly, I believe Ed suggests five to ten sessions with trained Theophostic ministers and then it's time to get booted from the nest and fly solo! In other words, you should be at the point where you can catch yourself overreacting to a situation, quickly get back to the root cause, uncover the lie and then ask Jesus to speak the truth. As far as I'm concerned, having a Theophostic moment is a much better choice than having all your church friends see you on the six o'clock news being hauled out of Walmart in handcuffs!

Most of the time when I make the effort, I am pretty good at being my own Theophostic coach, but if I get stuck in the muck, Ann and Trisha are still there for me. However, one night, my 'go-to-girls' weren't around and I found myself in dire straits. I was at the Friday night prayer meeting where months earlier I attended with Mary Ellen and Antoinette. The guy who played piano and led singing most weeks had captured my heart. His giftedness at the keyboard and beautiful singing voice often made it hard for me to focus on prayer. (The fact that he was really cute didn't help matters either.) I was so smitten by him I began to secretly fantasize that he would one day notice I existed and come to feel the exact same way about me. Tragically my dream was shattered when my friend Joan informed me that folks were starting to suspect he had something brewing with the gal who bi-monthly led the prayer meeting. (*Say it isn't so!*) As Joan was telling me this news over dinner one night I smiled and tried to fake happiness regarding this budding romance. But inwardly I was hoping the sparks would quickly fizzle and that she would promptly receive a call from God to join a convent!

Well anyway—on this particular Friday night, they were both part of the ministry team (Romeo at the piano—Juliet with her hands in the air leading us all before the throne). As I sat there ten feet away from the action, I began to have visions of their future life together. I imagined a huge Catholic wedding—she a raging beauty and he a stunning Prince Charming. I then saw them walking a beach in Hawaii, hand in hand, where they went for a three-week honeymoon. The next scene that flashed before my eyes included six beautiful, perfectly mannered Catholic angels, sitting at Mass with Mom and Dad. And finally, I was given a sneak preview of their 25th wedding anniversary celebration, neither of them having aged a day and still crazy in love with each other.

Meanwhile, back at the prayer meeting, I am now in a state of depression. (*Where's the Prozac?*) I remember thinking, *How come no one really cool ever wanted me?* Immediately I heard as clear as could be, "Because you're not attractive. You're just a loser." (***Ow!***) I was stunned. It felt like someone had just slugged me in the chest. As I sat there with tears welling up in my eyes, the last thing on my mind was, *Perhaps this might be a good time to do a little Theophostic.* But because I had done quite a bit of it, my mind just automatically went there. I began remembering awful moments during my teen years when mean and hurtful words were hurled at me by boys my age. I had been put down, shunned and rejected for not being pretty like the other girls. I was nothing but a chubby little tomboy from a broken home who never got asked to a single school dance. Memories of prom night came back. No one had asked me and instead of being off having the time of my life, I spent hours alone at the school yard, swinging on the swing set, feeling depressed and dejected. *Yep, I concluded, I sure am a loser!*

As tears rolled down my cheeks, somehow by God's grace I was able to ask the all-important question: *Jesus, is that true?*

If ever I heard with certainty the Lord speak, it was then and there. "Absolutely not. I adore you."

Although I wasn't raptured up to the mountain top for a hug session, Jesus made His presence known to me in that pew. As soon as He spoke those words, I had an amazing sensation of both His arms wrapped around me and of Him kissing the side of my head. That feeling remained for the duration of the prayer meeting. When the invitation came to go up for individual prayer, I didn't budge. There was no way I was leaving the Lord's embrace. The feeling lasted until the prayer meeting was over and it was time to go home.

Again, some may find what I just shared a bit too unorthodox and maybe even somewhat wacky. I get that. Still, for me it was real, and I shall never forget how happy I felt being enveloped in God's love that night. It was wonderful and if in sharing this my spiritual stability is questioned, so be it. If it makes you feel any better, my Theophostic moments are much less dramatic these days (perhaps because my over-reactions have been dialed down a bit). It's not that I don't still bonk out from time to time, but as I age I seem to have less energy for doing major drama.

Theophostic could be considered a form of mind renewal. With that being the case, I'll be doing it 'til the Lord returns or until He calls me home. The apostle Paul implored the Christians in Ephesus to be renewed in the spirit of their minds (Ephesians 4:23). For me that involves deleting infected files (removing lies) and downloading new programs (Biblical truth). Theophostic has been a great technique to have in my toolbox as it is structured, specific and effective. While I concede that not everyone had a childhood as turbulent as mine, I contend that not a single one of us got through our growing up years unscathed—which means we all have our recovery work cut out for us.

So, if you're feeling courageous and are ready to do some serious inner healing work, do a google search and try to connect with the Theophostic folks near you. And hey—if you run into problems and are coming up empty, just shoot me an e-mail. I still have Trisha's number on speed dial. I'll hook ya up!

Chapter 8

CATHOLICISM

On Ash Wednesday of 2009 I ventured into a Catholic Church to receive ashes. You might be wondering what possessed me to do such a thing and I confess—the motivation behind this endeavor was anything but spiritual (which stands to reason as I was still deep in sin). You see, there was this woman I was interested in who happened to be Roman Catholic and she invited me to participate in this yearly ritual with her. Truth be told I was so enamored with her I'd have gone to get a root canal together. Instead, she said to me, "Let's go get ashes!" to which I replied, "What a great idea. Count me in!"

What I knew about Catholicism I knew through my mom's mother and sister—Grama Zobie and Aunt Laurie. My mother left the Catholic church before I was born but Grama & Aunt La, as we affectionately called her, were diehard Catholics to the end. They regularly attended Mass, believed in purgatory, lit candles, thought all priests walked on water and were convinced that Mary was forever a virgin. Grama faithfully prayed the rosary and Aunt La was a regular patron in the confessional booth as she was quite a wild child well into her forties. Indeed, they were true blue, dyed-in-the-wool, cradle to grave Catholics. But neither of them knew Jesus. Both were presented with the gospel message before they departed from this earth and each willingly prayed the sinner's prayer. But I'm not sure if they actually understood what they were doing or if it was just one more ritual to perform in an attempt to cover all their religious bases. Sadly, despite their sincerity and loyalty to the Church, they didn't cast the Catholic faith in a very positive light and because of that I viewed all Catholics as being spiritually out to lunch.

So, there I was that afternoon—myself, full of iniquity but feeling righteous enough to cast judgment upon every person who walked into that church. I honestly expected to see most of them rush in, slap on those ashes and fly back out the door (burning rubber on their way out of the parking lot). Well, can you imagine my shock as I witnessed one person after another quietly enter, reverently receive their ashes and then sit down for a time of prayer?

Wait a minute—I thought I was at a Catholic Church. What are these people doing acting like this really matters to them and that they came to connect with God?

I kid you not, I was blown away by what was being played out before my eyes. We sat there for almost an hour and not a one of them lived up to my preconceived notions of how a

Catholic was supposed to behave. Admittedly—I found that to be rather disconcerting.

As my prejudices, one after another, blew up in my face, I was at a complete loss in knowing how to process this very strange occurrence. My friend, obviously sensing I was in a state of confusion, seized the moment by taking advantage of my vulnerable condition and suggested something that would forever change my life. She leaned over and whispered, "Would you like to come to Mass on Sunday?" I responded affirmatively with an enthusiastic headshake. "Yes, by all means—you bet I'll come to Mass!" The truth was, I needed more evidence to know if my anti-Catholic views were unfounded or if someone had simply slipped me some spiked ashes!

Much to my surprise I discovered that Mass was not a place where people went for an hour nap. Quite the opposite. It was a place of non-stop action, (not a single second to space out or check my email). Standing, bowing, kneeling, singing, praying, hand gesturing back and forth with the priest, slapping on holy water, filing forward to receive the Eucharist (in my case, a blessing) and occasionally sitting to catch my breath. Honestly, when it was all over, I was wiped out. Yet at the same time I felt exhilarated. Turning to my friend I smiled from ear to ear and told her, "That was awesome!" That's all it took. From then on, I was hooked and for six straight years I faithfully attended Mass—never out of obligation or duty, but rather out of pure joy. I couldn't wait to go.

"One thing have I desired of the Lord, that will I seek after; that I may dwell in the house of the Lord all the days of my life" (Ps. 27:4a KJV). This verse came alive for me as a practicing Catholic. Working most Sundays, I attended Mass Saturday evening and it soon became for me, date night with the Lord. I would get all dressed up and arrive at least an hour early in order to have the church mostly to myself for a while. I had downloaded many gospel songs on my phone, and once I popped in those ear buds, it was pure bliss! My hands were up in the air as I prayed, worshipped and communed with Jesus, having the absolute time of my life! Of course, this all had to be done in silence as to not upset the folks who had also arrived early to pray the rosary. But still, these times spent with God in His house were beyond wonderful and if anyone would have suggested I could be this happy sitting in a Catholic Church preparing my soul for Mass—I would have responded by asking, "What are you smokin'?"

Catholicism was in many ways like being in a foreign land. I grew up in a Baptist church and during my college days I journeyed over to the Pentecostal camp. My Baptist church passed out a bulletin every Sunday letting us know the order of worship, page numbers of the hymns we would be singing and the Scriptures to be read. The Pentecostal folks, on the other hand, were more into free style—allowing the Spirit to move anyway He chose to. ("WOO-HOO!") But at Mass, everything was spelled out (even the prayers). I never imagined myself being able to tolerate a worship service that was so structured but at this phase of my journey, knowing when to stand, when to sit, when to kneel, what responses were spoken and which ones were sung really appealed to me. I was in awe that everyone around me had the whole routine down—knowing exactly what to do and when to do it. I thought that was so cool. There was such a strong sense of unity as folks joined their voices together, whether the response was being spoken or sung. This was something I hadn't experienced as a Protestant; and wanting to be part of the oneness, I worked really hard to learn all the prayers and responses. (The ones that were lengthy and harder to memorize I wrote out on the blank pages in the back of my Bible.)

As best I can guess, knowing what to do and when to do it was a comfort to me simply because I had been on a wild ride for decades, never knowing what was going to hit me next. My life had been topsy-turvy—bouncing from church to church and relationship to relationship, with no stability whatsoever. I shall refrain from sharing the details of twelve failed relationships as it is irrelevant to the subject matter at hand. But recalling the details of my church wanderings would be quite beneficial (though totally embarrassing).

I was baptized a Methodist. Mom's Catholic mother and Dad's Methodist mom were more than likely warring over my soul and seeing how Dad was not a big fan of Catholicism, there was no way I'd be getting near the Catholic fount. There-fore, it was off to the Methodist church to be splashed in their waters, do a little screaming and appease both grandmamas. And that was it. My parents weren't interested in church so my stint as a Methodist lasted all of an hour. Years later I returned to the Methodist church after Grama Polhamus died but I only lasted a few months and then vanished once again (this time for good).

My earliest church memories are of Dad dropping us off and picking us up at an Episcopal Church. Ironically, I can't remember a single thing that went on there, only the car ride to and fro. My parents were no-shows except for an occasional appearance on Christmas or Easter but they made us kids go every week. We knew absolutely no one and were more than likely terrified being with all those strangers but like it or not, we went. I'm guessing that our grandmothers must have nagged, shamed and guilted our parents into sending us off on Sundays for fear that we would turn into heathens just like our parents. Thus, instead of watching cartoons, we spent each Lord's day hearing Bible stories at Sunday school. Unfortunately, when Dad left, so went the car and seeing how this church had no bus ministry, we could no longer attend. God, however, was watching out for us because soon thereafter some folks from the local Baptist church were canvasing our neighborhood. Mom invited them in and over coffee it was decided that my sisters and I would become Baptists. This church was also without a bus ministry but it was located a few blocks closer to our house with fewer busy streets to cross, so we were able to walk there.

I was an active, dedicated Baptist from 3rd grade until I went off to college. At the age of ten I went forward to receive Christ and was re-baptized a few months later on Easter Sunday, 1965. My heart was always hungry for God, but my understanding of Biblical truth lagged far behind. In the weeks leading up to being baptized my biggest worry was not about going under water but rather about all the sins from the others baptized before me floating around in the water. What if I picked up someone else's sin while in there and came out with them attached to me? (HORRORS!) For years I was perplexed with how on Earth I came up with that crazy thought because the washing away of one's sins in the baptismal waters is not what the Baptists teach about baptism. It is, however, what the Catholic Church believes (that baptism washes away original sin) and I have a strong suspicion that Grama and Aunt La were doing a little behind the scene catechesis on me. While I don't remember a specific conversation, it now makes sense that this is where my 'sins in the water' phobia originated.

Shortly after my baptism, I and all the other 5th graders at my church were presented a Bible. It was quite a thrill to receive such a gift and I still have memories of proudly marching home from church with it tucked under my arm. Unfortunately, I never read it. Being dyslexic, my reading skills were sub-par and the translation we were given (the Revised Standard Version) was not very reader friendly—especially for a ten-year old who read like a second grader. Therefore, the only Biblical knowledge I acquired came by listening to what was being taught in Sunday school. And being a kid who was easily distracted, not a whole lot was sinking in. Within my heart there was a sincere desire to follow Jesus but without the ability to read the Word and comprehend the truth of who God was and what was required of me as His follower, most of my Christian experience was based on feelings.

After high school I attended a liberal arts college in Michigan that was located in the middle of farm country. The nearest Baptist church was thirty miles away. Being accustomed to having church close by, the distance made it difficult for me to feel connected. That being the case I decided to stop attending church as no one seemed to care if I was there or not. This ill-fated decision resulted in my spiritual life taking a nosedive. Now that I was no longer accountable to a body of believers and a pastor, I pretty much did whatever I wanted and believe you me, I really pushed the envelope. Things however turned around the following fall, shortly into my sophomore year. In October of 1974 I entered the charismatic movement and my spiritually drained battery promptly received a mega charge. It was at this period in my life that I started to read the Bible—in fact I devoured it! A friend gave me a copy of the Living Bible and while not a very accurate translation, I could at least understand what I was reading. From the charismatics I moved over to the Pentecostal camp and quickly decided God was calling me to an Assembly of God Bible college. In hindsight, I was running away from my first homosexual relationship, hoping the move to Bible school would cure me. Sadly, it did not.

When I was twenty-eight, after years of battling against my romantic desires for women, I made my big 'gay proclamation'. That's when the roller coaster ride kicked into high gear. (Up until then it was just little bunny hills.) Unlike the current mindset of many evangelicals, when I came out, Bible believing Christians maintained that homosexuality was anything but 'gay'. It was viewed as sin—meriting immediate repentance. Sadly, even when repentant and seeking help, you were still shunned and rejected (which may explain why many older homosexuals are very bitter towards the Church).

Along the way I discovered a group of evangelical gay Christians. Those folks believed beyond a shadow of a doubt they were not only saved but that God was smiling upon their loving homosexual unions. And in fact, many of the individuals who were part of this group were in committed relationships—appearing stable, well-adjusted, favored and indeed, blessed. From them I learned how to reinterpret all the 'clobber passages', (verses condemning homosexuality). Once this new theology sank in, redefining what I had understood to be the truth concerning this forbidden behavior, I breathed a big sigh of relief. Deviating from the truth of Scripture never ends well. I immediately became delusional, convinced I could finally live a conviction free, guilt free, non-repentant, happy homosexual life. Problem was, happiness constantly eluded me and feeling convicted never ceased. But I did manage to stop repenting over my homosexual behavior. (What a big mistake that was.)

Considering myself to be an evangelical, I chose to attend Bible-believing churches. All would be well until homosexual sin was preached on. (Yes, thirty years ago ministers actually had the audacity to call out church attendees on the sin in their lives.) I was okay with sermons on sin as long as mine were off limits. But the minute sodomy was mentioned—that was it. (*Now you see me, now you don't!*) I would immediately depart and set sail in search of nicer Christians. As the years went by it became easier to find affirming 'gay friendly' churches but there was a tradeoff. Those who were okay with homosexual relationships had reached such a conclusion by watering down Biblical truth. (*Oh, dear.*) While I was happy about getting a pass on my immorality, my soul hungered for the deep things of God that were revealed in His Word. (I know, pretty crazy, eh?) So back and forth I went between orthodox churches and theologically relaxed congregations just like a little ping pong ball. Then, of course, there were all the gay churches popping up all over town. I checked out many of them but never lasted more than a month of Sundays as by then I was on everyone's nerves and they as well were driving me to drink. (We took dysfunction to a whole new level!)

So, that's my story—decades of instability concerning my church life. That's what made the Catholic Church and its rock-solid structure so appealing to me. After tossing all over the place for years on end, once I entered the Roman

Catholic system, I felt buckled in and secure. Having it all spelled out, knowing when to do what, and that the routine never changed—that worked for me. It was a safe place. If that seems strange and silly, oh well. I make no apologies because it was exactly what I needed.

Yet despite all the stability the Mass afforded me, there was still instability in my soul as my involvement with my new friend was intensifying. Week after week we sat together in church. If not for the humongous crucifix of Jesus that loomed directly in front of us, things would have been almost perfect. As messed up as my mind was and though my conscience was on life support, the constant visual of Jesus on the cross was causing me to squirm. Still, despite this weekly confrontation from on high, I kept right on being demented, believing I could manipulate the Lord into letting me have my way. I constantly told Him how grateful I was to have finally found the woman of my dreams and seeing how I had to persevere through eleven other relationships to finally get to the perfect one, perhaps He could cut me a little slack. (Okay—so maybe a lot of slack). But as it turned out, He wasn't about to budge an inch no matter how hard I tried to butter Him up with my self-serving gratefulness.

Being in such spiritual darkness, it wasn't sinking in that my sin of homosexuality was something Jesus had to atone for. In other words, that which I was claiming to be so grateful for and wanting God to put a stamp of approval on had put His Son on a cross—dying in my place—paying the debt I owed.

No amount of spinning or twisting Scripture into a pretzel was ever going to change that. And yet there I sat, week after week in arrogant defiance, deceiving myself into thinking I could enjoy the beauty of the Mass and the follies of sin all at the same time.

God tolerated this nonsense for six months and then the hammer came down. It was Labor Day weekend of 2009 when the amazing relationship I had been so enamored with blew up in my face. On the morning of my 54th birthday I raised the white flag of surrender—confessing my sin, repenting of my abominable behavior and pledging my absolute allegiance to the entire Word of God. From that day forward, I was a new creation in Christ (2 Cor. 5:17).

Two weeks prior to the imploding of this relationship, I signed up to join the Catholic Church, asking my friend to make the journey with me as a sponsor. No longer passengers on the love boat, we figured we could immediately hop on board the friendship train and continue on our merry way. Piece of cake, right? We would simply leave all the garbage behind us and move forward with our plans. That, however, was not a very wise decision. Although the physical relating had ceased, we were still emotionally entangled. In hindsight, a total break from one another would have been a much better option. But instead, we engaged in drama for the next twelve months.

As if relationship woes weren't enough to stress me out, there was also a theological storm brewing within. Ironically, once I repented of homosexual sin and came out of my spiritual coma, I emerged as an evangelical Protestant. (*OH, NO!*) I began listening to sermons on Christian radio all day long and for the first time in my life began to understand the doctrines of the Protestant faith. It didn't take very long before I was convinced that what I was hearing from the radio preachers was the gospel truth. Although I hadn't been introduced to the five Solas of the Reformation, Sola Scriptura was already in my heart. My commitment to Scripture alone was non-negotiable as I was ever aware of the damage that had been inflicted on my soul by deviating from it. As good as this all was, it set me on a collision course with the Catholic Church. I was in the process of hitching my wagon to her, despite being in complete alignment with the teaching of Martin Luther and John Calvin. What was I thinking? That's just it—I wasn't thinking. It was all about **feeling**. Catholicism satisfied something deep within my heart and regardless of all my doctrinal misgivings, the magnet pulling me towards Rome rendered me completely helpless to all logic. At the time, I had no idea what it was that made me run into the arms of this church. It would take leaving and getting into therapy to figure it out.

Because my emotions were running the show, I comprehended very little of what I was being taught on Catholic doctrine. The little I did grasp—such as the Marian dogmas, the supremacy of the Pope, the Eucharist being the actual body and blood of Jesus and purgatory caused me great concern. Once my instructors figured out I wasn't embracing these doctrines they suggested I delay my coming into the church. That made perfect sense and I should have thanked them for everything and graciously bowed out. Instead, I had a total meltdown. I cried my heart out and felt like my world was coming to an end! The following evening I limped into my prayer room, desperately needing to hear from Jesus. As I began to read my Bible, one passage of Scripture after another started to jump right off the page. Those verses spoke powerfully to me, and before long, all the fear and anxiety that for months had been plaguing my heart concerning Catholicism, vanished! I ended up on my knees, sobbing, feeling wave after wave of love washing over me. God's presence was never more real to me and, when all was said and done, I felt as if I had been given permission to join the church—that it was heavens gift to me (and in many ways it was).

For the first three years, I was on cloud nine. As long as I could put a Protestant spin on Catholic doctrine, Catholicism worked for me. I was making wonderful new friends, falling more deeply in love with Jesus with every passing day and grateful beyond words for the abundance of grace afforded to me as a member of the Roman Catholic Church. Sadly, my bliss was disrupted as I began learning more of what I was required to believe as a Catholic. For example, I thought all the grace I was receiving via the sacraments was helping me toward sanctification, not justification. I had no idea that in Catholicism you aren't considered justified until you've actually reached a state of perfection, attaining righteousness within yourself. Protestants on the other hand believe we are righteous the moment we put our faith in the substitutionary death of Christ on the cross, thus receiving His righteousness. Martin Luther referred to it as an alien righteousness. (*How'd I miss that not-so-minor detail?*) There were other things that began to trouble me as well such as the Mass being a bloodless sacrifice, lighting candles for the deceased, having Mass offered up for relatives in Purgatory and more revelations on just how powerful Mary was. To expound on the theological issues dividing Catholics and Protestants is the subject for another book (which I don't plan to write). Suffice it to say, this new information began clogging up my Protestant filter to the point where it stopped working—making me seriously question if I should remain in the Church. The joy I felt vanished and anxiety began to plague my soul.

For the remainder of my days as a practicing Catholic I was conflicted. My heart wanted to stay but my brain was telling me I had to go. The people who were closest to me knew I was in turmoil and did their best to help. Joan would explain to me that Catholicism held the fullness of truth. Ann would just pray with me. (Amazingly, she didn't tell me I needed to do Theophostic!) I would often share my doubts with Fr. Richard when I went to confession and more than once he was able to keep me from jumping overboard. But no amount of reasoning, praying, or forgiveness from my priest was sufficient when it came to ridding me of the uneasiness within because deep down I knew I was not a believer of Roman Catholicism. (That was the sin I should have confessed when I went to confession—that I was flying under false colors.) When I finally had the courage to own up to being Protestant, I knew I could no longer march in the Catholic army and share the Eucharist with them. Thus, with great sadness and a broken heart, I left the Church I loved and returned to my Protestant roots.

Since leaving I have often pondered the experience I had in my prayer room the night I believed God was giving me the 'A-Okay' to enter the Catholic Church. I admit to playing fast and loose with my Bible as I randomly flipped from one passage to the next—isolating verses without reading them in the context in which they were written. But still, every single passage seemed to point me towards Rome. Was it my desperation that caused me to bend Scripture into saying what I wanted to hear so I could do what I wanted to do? Perhaps that was the case. Yet there's something within that still believes the Catholic Church was God's gift to me—if only for a season. Could it be that God in His omniscience drew me to the Church where I would mend and heal? Is it possible that providence led me to Joan Darcy who would point me in the direction of Unbound? Might it be too farfetched to contend that before one of my days came to be, my heavenly Father ordained an encounter with Mary Ellen—sending me to Shepherd's Group where I'd meet an angel named Ann who would do Theophostic with me? "All the days ordained for me were written in your book before one of them came to be" (Psalm 139:16 NIV). Were Debbie, Craig, Agnes, Colleen, Jim, Phil and Fr. Richard part of the gift I had been given that special night? Or is it my stubborn pride that won't allow me to own that I made it all up? I guess you'll have to draw your own conclusions.

There is hardly a day that goes by that I don't miss the Catholic Church. I confess—there have even been times when I've asked the Lord if there is a way back for me. But the answer is always the same, "There is not." While I have more peace in my heart, no longer wrestling with dogmas that violate my conscience, I have continual sadness—grieving the loss of a church I loved so deeply. Yet, amidst the sadness, I feel an immense amount of gratitude. It was the Catholic Church that took me in when I was lost and broken, providing a safe haven for me to recover. Amidst the candles, statues, incense and a multitude of rosaries, I was set free and restored to my right mind. If not for all the love pouring into me day after day, month after month for six plus years as I journeyed life's path in the Catholic community, I honestly don't know if I'd have gotten well. And in all honesty, that thought haunts me.

Chapter 9

THERAPY

For about the last year and a half as a practicing Roman Catholic I began visiting Protestant churches. I would attend Mass on Saturday night and as my work schedule allowed, hang out with the evangelicals on Sunday morning. The thought of leaving the Catholic Church not only filled my heart with sadness but also had me feeling scared. What if I was indeed walking away from 'the one, true church' (as I had been told again and again)? Was I about to make a terrible decision that I'd spend all of eternity lamenting over? Thus, not being 100% sure of my soul's final destination, I would corner the pastor as soon as the service ended and unload my Catholic dilemma on him. I'd tell them him much I loved being Catholic but didn't believe anything they taught that conflicted with Protestant doctrine. I think I was desperately looking for someone to give me permission to leave. But most of them would just smile, tell me I was welcome to attend their services any time and sidestep weighing in on Catholic doctrine (perhaps because they concluded they were dealing with someone who didn't have both oars in the water). While I appreciated the open invitation for fellowship, they did little to help me resolve my predicament. And then I met Pastor Floyd.

Pastor Floyd and I sat down together in May of 2015 to discuss the conflict I was experiencing concerning Catholicism. He was one of the pastors at a Protestant church in Detroit I had been attending for a couple of months. He listened as I laid out the Catholic doctrines that were short circuiting my Baptist brain and in no time flat correctly assessed that my faith was more in alignment with the Reformers than with the Magisterium of the Roman Catholic Church. But as soon as he outed me as a Protestant, I began lamenting over how much I loved being Catholic and that the thought of leaving was tearing me up inside.

At this point Pastor Floyd looked at me kind of funny and said, "I think your problem is more emotional than intellectual."

That stood to reason as it had been my heart, overruling my brain, that sent me there in the first place. His advice was short but not so sweet. "Cry your tears and make your move." (*Goodness gracious!*) Before we parted, he prayed for me and it was right up there with, "cry your tears." Pastor Floyd prayed the Lord would give me no rest until I left the Catholic Church. (What a fun time that turned out to be.)

When I ran into Pastor Floyd a couple weeks later he asked me where I was at in regard to our conversation.

"Oh, I've been telling my friends that I'm going to leave," I replied, hoping he would think I was making great progress.

"But have you left?" he wanted to know.

Oh, for crying out loud—of course I haven't left! I'm just going to talk about it for the next ten years! That would have been the honest thing to say but instead I smiled and sweetly said, "Not yet, Pastor Floyd."

I was beginning to regret ever having met with him. Why couldn't he be like all those other nice ministers and tell me to take all the time I needed—to be undecided 'til the cows came home, the fat lady sang, or the Lord returned to settle the matter once and for all? I tried avoiding him when at church but that didn't work because he popped up everywhere. He had prayed God would give me no rest until I left the Catholic Church and then decided to be the Lord's chosen vessel in driving me out of my mind! I obsessed for days over how to get out of the pickle I was in, all the while knowing Pastor Floyd was absolutely right and the only option that would give me peace was to honor my convictions, obey my conscience and actually leave. So, I mustered up all the strength within me and immediately stopped going to Mass. Six weeks later I went back to Mass and immediately stopped hanging out with the Protestants.

All was bliss for two months until I slammed into another brick wall, making it painstakingly clear I had to leave and this time, for good. One Thursday night at a prayer meeting I faithfully attended it was suggested that every morning we should come to the Father and ask Him what He had for us that day. I thought that was a great idea. We were also encouraged to ask the same thing of Jesus and again, I was totally onboard. And finally, we were told to go to the Blessed Mother—asking her the same thing. (*Time out!*)

The thought of asking Mary every morning what she had in store for me sent a shiver down my spine as I felt the Blessed Mother had just been made part of the eternal Godhead. I wanted to pack up my Bible and run out the door. Had there not been several new folks at the prayer meeting that night, I might have done just that: BOLTED! But for the sake of the first-time visitors, I forced myself to sit still and not cause a scene (even though I was on the verge of losing it). Of course, suggesting a morning check in with Mary was really not that out of the ordinary. I had met many Catholics who did that regularly as they had consecrated themselves to her. I don't know—maybe I just couldn't take it anymore which is why by the end of the prayer meeting I was coming unglued. After the meeting ended, our leader, who sensed that the Mary suggestion had not set well, asked me about it. I replied the way I always did when tripped up by something other Catholics were fine with.

"This isn't Biblical!" To which I heard the usual response that I had heard again and again and again;

"Catholics also believe in Tradition."

That was the last straw. New folks or not, I couldn't contain my anger. "Well I'm a really rotten Catholic," I confessed loudly! And with that I stormed out the door, never to return.

After my exodus from the Catholic Church and return to the Protestant camp, I was constantly running to the altar after the Sunday morning service for prayer as I felt a tremendous sense of loss. While I struggled with doctrine, there was a rich vastness I experienced as a Roman Catholic and I was missing that. I was grieving the loss of having served as a Cantor, Eucharistic Minister and Lector. Giving interviews on Catholic radio and sharing my story at various venues came to a screeching halt! Not having any opportunity to use my gifts and tell my story left me feeling benched and totally dejected. Struggling against a major plunge into depression I also made use of a free counseling service run by lay persons at the church I was attending. But much to my disappointment neither the altar folks nor the lay counsellors were able to alleviate the sorrow, confusion and guilt I felt for leaving the Catholic Church. I had let down my Catholic friends and all the folks who had poured into my life, helping me recover and regain my sanity. (What a traitor I turned out to be!) I was a mess and it was pretty apparent I needed professional help to sort things out, but I didn't see how I could possibly afford it. So, I continued to seek out more free services in hopes of getting much needed answers. What was it that drew me to the Catholic Church even though I knew I didn't believe much of what they taught? What made me go back after I left? What was it about leaving the Catholic Church that had me feeling sorrow in the very depths of my soul? I feared if I didn't get some clarity and figure things out, I would go back again (and then leave again). I kept asking myself, *What if I keep repeating this cycle till my days on Earth have ended and then die in a state of total confusion?* Filled with anxiety over this being my fate, I bit the bullet and scheduled an appointment with a Biblical counselor.

Because I was a woman on a tight budget, I showed up at my first appointment engines blazing, hoping to sort everything out in record breaking time (two weeks—three max). There wasn't a moment to waste on the trivial—we needed to get right to the heart of the matter within the first five minutes of session one. Having a B.A. in counseling psychology, I wrote up my own intake evaluation ahead of time—identifying my issues, their root causes and how much progress I had made in overcoming these psychological shortcomings. The minute I walked through the door I handed it to my therapist. (Okay, we might of said, "Hello", but not much else.) I made it very clear that my goal in being there was to deal with my attachment to the Catholic Church, (I think I wrote that in big letters, all capitalized on my intake evaluation) and the quicker I got answers for that, the sooner I'd be on my way. Well much to my dismay, we began discussing my relationship with my father. (*WHAT?!?*) How we got on that topic I can't for the life of me remember. I probably said something snarky about him (which was a fatal move on my part) and thus, Dad became the focus. I quickly tried to get us back on track, zooming in on the reason for my visit but the conversation went right back to me and dear old dad. (*Kill me now!*)

I sat there seething as we wasted my precious dollars on subject matter completely irrelevant to the crisis at hand. *Good grief, isn't it enough that I subject myself to nightly irritations via phone calls, to make sure he and my stepmother are alright? Now I have to fork out money to sort through this aggravating relationship? Really? Oh, come on! I'm here to talk about Catholicism! Why are we talking about my dad? There's been a mistake—A GREAT BIG ONE! Are we really going to pick apart my relationship with my father and blow up my Visa in the process?*

Yep. That's exactly what we were going to do.

Chapter 10

DAD

I f ever there was a little girl who was crazy about her father, I was that child. The best part of my day was when Dad's car pulled in the driveway, returning him home to us after work. If I was down the street playing with friends, I would immediately bolt for home screaming, "DAD" the whole way. It was always a glorious reunion as I would jump into his arms and then cling to him the rest of the night. My mother had lots of competition from me, vying for Dad's affection. After the evening meal each night Mom and Dad had 'hug and kiss time'. Being only six years old, I had no concept of other people's boundaries (still working on that one in my sixties) so there I'd be, climbing up his back, wanting him to pay attention to me. My poor parents. Looking back, I wonder why they didn't lock me up some-where after supper, so they could share some tender moments in peace. But they never did (even though I'm pretty sure it crossed their minds).

My father was very devoted to his daughters. He read to us, gave us piggyback rides to bed each night, tucked us in and always verbalized how much he loved us. Dad made sure his girls had all the essentials that kids needed for a happy childhood such as bicycles and baseball gloves for summer fun plus sleds and ice skates to have a blast in the winter. Of course, we also had dolls, play dishes and other girly treasures but seeing how my favorite playmate was Dad, I was more inclined to put those things aside and grab my baseball mitt.

Our Christmases were totally outrageous. The living room looked like a photo shoot from the Montgomery Ward's Christmas Catalog. As kids, we had no appreciation of how hard Dad worked to lavish us with such treasures, but the old black and white photos from childhood, showing mountains of gifts under the tree, made it crystal clear. We were definitely his little darlings and December 25th was a perfect occasion to express how much he adored us.

Our father was also top notch when it came to taking my sisters and me to fun places. I can still remember trips to Camp Dearborn, Kent Lake and going to Detroit Tiger baseball games. A few miles from our house there was an amusement park called Edgewater where we were frequent patrons. It was always such a thrill to go there (in spite of the fact that I was too scared to go on most of the rides). One evening my sister talked me into going on the Wild Mouse with her. (The Wild Mouse was a baby roller coaster.) As we began our approach to the first bunny hill I started to scream,

"I want off!" I was having such a hissy fit that our dad made them stop the ride so I could be rescued! Yet despite my meltdown on the Wild Mouse, I was fearless when it came to flying down snow covered hills on my sled. One year Dad got us a toboggin for Christmas which was a total riot—that is until we ran it into a tree. I was in front and my sister, the 'Wild Mouse Queen', was sitting behind me. When she knew we were doomed to crash, she jumped off. I must have had my eyes closed on the way down the hill because I took the tree head on. Our father, who was at the top of the hill raced down to where I was and pulled me up that slick, snow packed hill as I laid on the toboggin screaming my head off. I wasn't hurt, just scared. Wow! What a hero Dad was that day.

All year round we could count on trips to the corner drug store for an ice cream cone. Decades before there were Baskins Robbins, family owned drug stores were the place folks went for an ice cream treat. For thirty-five cents you got a huge scoop of your favorite flavor on a sugar cone. There were outings to the Dairy Queen as well. But seeing how Dad loved butter pecan ice cream, I have many more memories of us at Green's Drug Store, licking away at chocolate ice cream on a sugar cone.

Yes indeed! We sure did have an awesome dad. But like all fallen children of Adam, he had a dark side. My father could not control his temper and more than once became physically abusive to my mother. Sadly, their marriage was somewhat of a train wreck from the get-go and I marvel that it lasted as

long as it did. Mom and Dad met in a bar where Mom was
the hat check girl and Dad occasionally sang. Back in the day,
my mother was an absolute knock out and Dad, of course,
took notice. They both liked to drink and they both loved to
sing. Mom's dream was to be in show biz. In her late teens, she
worked at a club in Detroit with Rosemary Clooney, where the
two of them became chums. When Mom heard Dad sing, she
had visions of their names in lights as they crooned the country-
side together! But that never panned out. Shortly after getting
married, Dad put the kibosh on Mom's dream of stardom, and
so instead of becoming performers, they had babies and became
parents. And of course, they continued to drink.

A couple of years into their marriage my father, having had
way too many, flew into a drunken rage. He decided he was
leaving and that he was taking his one-year old daughter with
him (the 'designated driver', no doubt). As he tossed her in the
back seat of his car, my grandmother (Grama Zobie) started
screaming for someone to come and save my sister. One of the
neighbors jumped into action, subduing Dad until the police
came to haul him off to the slammer. The next morning when
my father woke up behind bars he rightly assessed he had acted
very foolishly and decided right then and there to never take
another drink. He maintained his sobriety for the rest of his
days on Earth, dying four days after his 65-year AA anniversary.

Mom, however, having no 'jail cell awakening', continued
drinking. Dad tried very hard to get her to quit, doing everything he could think of. He took her to AA meetings with

him, dumped out her hidden beer bottles (sometimes on her head), lectured, begged, pleaded, and when all else failed, he hit. There were times I would stand ten feet away and watch it all play out before my innocent eyes. My sister, on the other hand, being four years older and wiser, knew the moment was right to be wild little hoodlums. During their brawls she'd grab me by the arm and pull me into their bedroom where we'd play trampoline on the bed, jumping our stress away. A day or two later, after they had kissed and made up, we'd all gather round the piano to sing songs from Rogers and Hammerstein musicals. (I'm not making this up.) The biggest tragedy of all was that reality television wasn't around. We'd have been a shoe in for our own series!

Having a father with anger issues took a toll on all of us. As much as I adored my dad, I feared him in a way no child should fear their daddy. I lived with constant anxiety—trying ever so hard not to tick him off because I believed if I did, it might be the end of me. Once, when I was about eight or nine years old, I was playing in Dad's car when suddenly the car started rolling backwards down the driveway. I had no idea what I had done but knew enough to put my foot on the brake. The boy next door was in his front yard and hearing my cries for help came to the rescue, putting the car back in park. Well, I immediately knew I was in a heap of trouble and after quickly weighing my options decided to run and hide. Jumping out of the car I made a mad dash from the scene of the crime and took off down the street as fast as my little legs could carry me. Running for my life, fearing Dad would soon be chasing after me, I franticly searched for a safe hide-a-way. With my heart pounding and my lungs about to explode I made a split-second decision to duck into Mrs. Dwellie's yard and barricade myself behind her garage. (Mrs. Dwellie lived two houses down from us.) Gasping for air I whispered aloud, "He'll never find me here!"

But before I had a chance to formulate survival plans for my new life behind our neighbor's garage I heard,

"ROBIN!" I froze and held my breath.

"ROBIN!" It was Dad calling.

"Horrors!" I quietly cried, "I'm doomed!"

"ROBIN!"

Obviously, he noticed his car had changed location and that Mom's white picket fence from Kmart, completely demolished by the open car door, lay in shambles on the lawn. (*Yikes!*)

"ROBIN!"

I tried to ignore him for as long as I could but after holding out for the longest three minutes of my life, I slowly began the death march home to suffer my fate.

Dad and I had our confrontation in the garage where he was fixing something or other. He had a wrench in his hand and while I don't remember how big that wrench actually was, to my nine-year-old eyes it appeared lethal. I began to plead for my life. "Dad, please don't hit me with the wrench," I sobbed!

That is one of the saddest memories of my life. I'm 100% sure the thought never occurred to him to whack me in the head with that tool but the mere fact I considered it a possibility—how tragic. The person God placed in my life to be my refuge and protector—the one I loved and adored with all my heart had become someone I feared might very well end my life.

As their marriage continued to implode my parents reached a place of desperation and eventually decided to talk to the pastor at the Episcopal church where they sent us girls each week. Mom and Dad agreed to a temporary separation so things could cool down and they could both regroup. I have blocked out the moment when Dad left, but knowing me, I probably had a major meltdown as he had never been away from us except to go to work. While I don't cognitively remember Dad's words, I remember them emotionally.

"I'll be back."

But during that time of separation, Mom decided she had had enough of his abuse and filed for divorce. Upon breaking the news to me she uttered four words that totally shattered my world: "Dad's not coming back."

I don't recall what I said to my mother in reply (if anything) but I absolutely remember what happened next. I walked out of the house, stood in our front yard, looked up at the sky and asked, "God, why my parents? Out of all the kids in the world, why **my** mom and dad?"

Looking back, it seems pretty apparent that already by age seven my understanding of a compassionate, merciful

God was shaky at best. In that moment of sorrow when I desperately needed comfort from the One who loved me most, I felt totally alone and completely betrayed. As far as I was concerned, God had become the great big meanie up in the sky who dished out awful stuff on unsuspecting little kids. And for some reason, unbeknown to me, He decided that my family should be blown up. Although I didn't verbalize any anger, there's no doubt in my mind that I was pretty ticked off at Him for doing such a thing. It never occurred to me that I should be mad at my stupid parents. Years later I would indeed be livid with both of them. But in that moment—I viewed almighty God as the enemy.

It never ceases to amaze me when folks from broken homes tell me the divorce of their parents had little ill effect on them. I literally scratch my head because as I shared earlier, I was absolutely devastated when Mom and Dad split. Perhaps when ex-spouses remain amicable towards one another for the sake of their children it helps ease the pain. Sadly, my parents were anything but. Every time Dad came over to the house, World War 3 broke out. The hitting had ceased but not the yelling and arguing. They couldn't be in the same room for more than five minutes without getting into it. On one occasion, there was breaking glass and lots of blood. That particular night, Mom attempted to throw Dad out of the house by pushing closed the back door on him. Dad continued to hurl insults at her from his side of the door and didn't seem to be in a hurry to go anywhere until he was finished belittling her. That made Mom all the angrier and more determined to get rid of him by locking the door. She continued to push hard on the door but because she was so angry and not thinking straight, her hand was applying pressure on the windowpane rather than the wood. Well, you can guess what happened next. Her arm went through the glass, causing a deep gash from her wrist to her elbow. My sisters and I were horrified! My father's response was to laugh and call her "Smarty". He did, however, take her to the hospital to get stitched up and even replaced the glass on the back door. (What a guy.) That was the only trip to the emergency room, but the verbal battles continued for many years beyond that.

Dad didn't like being alone and eventually remarried. I, for one, was happy to have a stepmother and Dad's new wife seemed thrilled to have acquired three daughters. She delved right into her new role as our stepmommy, showering us with gifts, affection and in no time at all had positioned herself at the helm, setting sail for new waters. That didn't go over too well with Mom, who let Dad's new gal know in no uncertain terms that she was our mother "so back off, Toots!" Needless to say, our new stepmother was deeply hurt when Mom backed her off. I believe she meant well, and must have felt very rejected. Unfortunately, she didn't handle the situation with much class and in turn decided (perhaps unconsciously) that if she couldn't be the mom, Dad wouldn't be the dad! (*Seriously?*) My sisters and I spent the rest of our childhood caught in the middle of a battle between two deeply wounded women who had mega insecurities. (Dad sure knew how to pick 'em!)

My father hated conflict and avoided confrontations at all cost. So rather than making the effort to remain committed to his daughters as a faithful father, we were escorted from the ship and relegated to occasional guest passengers. Eventually, we referred to ourselves as our father's 'stepdaughters'. But in all honesty, we became 'ex-daughters'. Along with my mother, we had been divorced.

Dad and his new wife wanted to have children. After losing their first baby within minutes of being born, they gave birth to a second son on October 1st, 1970. I was fifteen at the time, just starting high school. Dad had a family again and all the love and affection he once gave us was now showered upon his son. My brother Bernie was born with a defective heart which necessitated even more love and care than had he arrived on the planet up to snuff. I could fill pages and pages with examples of all the hurtful incidents where the underlying message that was implanted in my mind was *Bernie rocks! You Girls? Not so much.* But this chapter is already enough of a downer without dredging up all those memories. Suffice it to say, it cut like a knife, caused a lot of emotional damage and will keep me doing Theophostic until Jesus returns.

I carried into adulthood many ill feelings towards my father. My heart was plagued with bitterness for the way he dropped the ball, kicked us to the curb and could never acknowledge any of the hurtful things he had done. But amazingly, the little girl inside of me never stopped loving him and longing for his return. Even after he married my stepmother and had my brother, I held out hope he and Mom would get back together again. It wasn't until sitting at my mother's funeral that I finally let go of that pipe dream. (I was one month shy of twenty-six.)

Right up to the end of Dad's life I kept actively campaigning for the return of his heart. Although we had moments along the way when the dad of yesteryear resurfaced, the encounters were brief and very sporadic. He'd quickly revert back to Bernie's dad and my stepmother's husband, breaking my heart yet one more time. Through the years Dad would make a promise, then break a promise because my stepmother would object whenever he wanted to do something for us. That scenario was repeated often and one would think I'd have wised up along the way. But I never did. Whatever Dad was selling, I was buying, only to end up hurt, disappointed and angry. While we did this dance 'til his death, the dad of my childhood showed up a few more times before he went home to be with the Lord.

My father was diagnosed with prostate cancer in 1998. Deciding to trust God for healing, he ignored every one of his doctor's suggestions for treatment and took supplements instead. For sixteen years his cancer was a non-issue until 2014 when it showed up in his bones. It was then that he decided to let God heal him with the aid of modern medicine. The treatments zapped Dad of most of his energy, but he was still able to remain in his house with my stepmother and their dog, Suzie. In May of 2017 he was rushed to the hospital where they discovered he was septic caused by an infected gallbladder. Dad never again returned home, spending the last four months of his life going back and forth between the hospital and the rehab center/nursing home. My stepmother did not come to see him a single time, stating she was too ill to get out of the house. Looking back, I believe it was her undiagnosed anxiety disorder that kept her homebound and unable to be with her life-mate of fifty years. But at the time it was happening, I for one lacked compassion. I wasn't seeking to understand what was really going on with her. It was much easier to be angry and judgmental for doing such a thing to my father. Yet as peeved as I was, I admit to also being pretty happy she wasn't around. (Okay—thrilled!)

With Dad's wife not on the scene I had a better chance of getting back the dad I once knew. (How pathetically selfish and sinful on my part for feeling that way.) Granted, it wasn't all bliss as my dear stepmother didn't totally disappear. She was still able to run the planet via telephone. She called my father and the nursing home a zillion times a day and could mess with his head even over the phone. But in all fairness, while it has been my tendency to blame everything on her, Dad could be hurtful all on his own without any help from his wife. Nevertheless, mingled in with the chaos, drama and smack-downs, we had some special times near the end of his life that deeply touched my heart.

Dad loved to sing and continued crooning right to the end—singing songs to the nursing home staff just days before he made his transition. So, during one of my visits I asked Dad if he wanted to sing and he thought that was a good idea. Anticipating a fun time singing duets together I hurried out to my car to fetch my iPod and Bose speaker. But our sing along quickly turned into my serenading him. He sang half a song with me then stopped, seeming more content to just lie in bed and listen to his daughter.

Dad had a great ear for music and would comment when he thought I had done a good job arranging a song (which put me on cloud nine). I continued singing song after song and then something very strange happened. I was singing Edelweiss from The Sound of Music when Dad started to cry (and we're not talking tears running down his cheeks—it was a full blown, 'boo hoo'). I had to look out the window as seeing my father cry had me on the verge of losing it. When the song ended, I asked Dad what was up. I half expected him to say, "I don't know," which was his usual response when it came to talking about his feelings. But he didn't. He immediately started talking about the afternoon back in March of 1965 when he took me to see the movie. He reminisced how mesmerized I was the entire time and the profound impact it had on my life. He recalled buying me the album and how that movie forever changed my life. I sat there with my jaw on the floor, eyes bulging out of my head, absolutely blown away by the words coming out of his mouth.

He remembered it all so perfectly—as if we'd gone to see the movie just the other day—not fifty plus years prior! But not only did he still remember—the memory of it had him crying half a century later. (*Okay, who are you and what have you done with my father?*)

One of the things every daughter needs from her daddy is to be affirmed in her appearance by having her dad compliment how she looks. My dad never did that, and I eventually resigned myself to the fact he either thought I was an ugly duckling or just plain didn't notice me. Then one day out of the blue he complimented my outfit—specifically mentioning the color combinations I had put together and how much he liked my striped blouse. That comment thrilled me so much I smiled the entire way home. When I showed up the next week it got even better. Dad told me my outfits were so cool I could model them. During that drive home I contemplated scheduling a photo shoot with Vogue but then remembered Dad was on round the clock narcotics so perhaps my outfits weren't all that dazzling. I didn't care. Dad thought I looked good, so as far as I was concerned, they could keep them drugs a comin'! But what took the cake was a phone conversation we had exactly one week before he died. I called him on the way to work and while we were doing our usual chit chatting, out of the blue he asked, "What are you wearing today?"

I described my outfit and he then went off on how sharp I dressed and how nice it was to see a woman that took care of herself. Dad then wanted to know if I ever wore dresses.

"I sure do, Dad and one of these days I'm going to wear one for you."

Sadly, he died before I could make good on that promise. But I dressed to the hilt for his funeral—hat and all. (He would have loved that outfit, drugs or no drugs!)

The last time Dad and I were together we talked about my brother Bernie being his favorite. He of course denied it, claiming he loved us all equally. I remained unconvinced but knew he wasn't going to be swayed into admitting it, so I changed the subject. However, later that evening after I fed Dad and was getting ready to leave, I revisited the 'favorite child' topic one more time. Regardless of what Dad said, my brother had captured Dad's heart in a way his daughters never could. Did it bother me that there was a special child and it wasn't me? Obviously, it did, otherwise I would have kissed him goodbye and walked out the door. But instead I had to ask him one more question.

"Okay, Dad—so you loved us all the same." (*Whatever.*) "But out of all us kids, who was most crazy about you?"

Not missing a beat, he immediately replied, "You, Rob. When I'd come home from work, there you'd be with your baseball glove on, standing in the driveway, waiting for me."

Hearing him say that brought satisfaction to my heart. Although I wasn't the most loved child, I was the one who loved the most and at the end of the day, what's better than that?

My father went to be with the Lord on September 9th, 2017 and although I had just turned 62 a few days prior to that, I once again became a little girl. All day long my heart cried out, *DAD!* As I rode my bike that afternoon I even said it aloud. "DAD!" Towards the end of his life I was reawakened to the first love I had for my father. The little girl who had anxiously awaited his return home each night reappeared. For years I had done everything possible to get that man out of my heart but all I really succeeded in doing was to put up walls in an attempt to protect myself from further hurt and brokenness. When it was all said and done, I found myself standing amidst the rubble—heart exposed—once again loving my Earthly father to the core of my being. And all the tears I couldn't cry the first time he left gushed out like a waterfall the day he departed for glory.

Why is it that God places some children in homes with amazing dads and others end up with fathers who miss the mark? I don't know the answer to that one. But whatever the reason, I no longer believe it's because God loves some of us less than the kids who were given awesome dads. No way. If anything, He may even love us more. Now I realize there are no specific verses in Scripture to substantiate this, but, somehow, I feel like the fatherless have a special gig with God that children from really happy homes may not be privy to. "Even when my father and mother abandon me, the Lord will hold me close" (Ps. 27:10 NLT). "The Lord will take me in" (ESV). "The Lord will take me up" (KJV).

Someday I shall be reunited with the man I once called 'Dad'. But when we meet again, he will no longer be my dad, but rather, my brother. Until that day, I am traveling the remainder of the journey home in the arms of God, who gives me the joy of calling **Him**, 'Father'. The guy I loved and adored in this life, who long ago hauled me up an icy hill, rescued me from the Wild Mouse and carried me on his back to bed at night—I won't call him 'Dad' ever again (in spite us having knowledge of our earthly relationship). For all of eternity I will be relating to him as my brother in Christ and calling him by perhaps a new name that the Lord has given him. But I'm okay with that and this is the reason why. The One who created me, redeemed me, healed me, gave me life eternal and adopted me into His family—He is now, has always been and forever will be my Abba! Therein lies my hope. Therein lies my joy. Therein lies my everything!

Chapter 11

MOM

Writing about my mother will be more difficult than it was to crank out page after page on Dad because she died before I really had the chance to know and understand who she was. (Mom was only fifty-two when she passed.) There wasn't enough time to analyze the deep inner workings of her psyche and to figure out what made her tick, as had been the case with my father. She was taken from us much too soon! But the bigger reason I will struggle in writing about her is because I don't want to expose her flaws as it will only add to the feelings of guilt I already bear surrounding her death. You see, by the time I reached my teens our relationship had deteriorated to the point that I just wanted to get away from her. I had longings of being adopted into a nice family—having parents that could express love. The only way that would ever happen was if she died. In my selfish, sin infected, evil heart, I remember times of wishing it would happen. A decade later that wicked wish came true. By then things were much better between us and her death was, and still is, a terrible loss for me. I suppose on some level I fear that perhaps my wish contributed to her untimely death. So, having killed off my poor mother, how dare I dig up her past sins and trash her legacy! But if I'm to give an honest assessment of how our relationship contributed to my inordinate desires, then I have to do it.

My mother was born in October of 1928. Aunt La, her only sibling, came along twenty months later. Grampa Zobie was an Irish immigrant and true to his heritage, he was a drinker. According to my aunt, their daddy was a falling-down drunk and by the time Mom was seven, he managed to drink himself right into his grave. Mom rarely talked about her dad. Most of what I know about him came from Aunt La—and those conversations usually took place on nights when she was 'three sheets to the wind'. Aunt La claimed that Grampa, during a drunken rage, once beat the tar out of my mother—which may shed some light on why she married an abusive husband and stayed with him for more than a decade. This is what she knew and, probably on some level, felt she deserved. Sadly, as my mother's alcoholism progressed, she as well became abusive to her daughters—verbally, emotionally and physically. And we in turn, were at times brutal to one another. (The Waltons we were not!)

Aunt La, like her father, was also a 'falling-down drunk'. But unlike Grampa Zobie, she wasn't violent or abusive after consuming too much alcohol. She was actually a barrel of laughs when she got bombed—even when sprawled out in the middle of our living room floor. Mom on the other hand rarely got intoxicated, no matter how much she drank. Over the years she simply morphed into a depressed alcoholic, consuming six or more beers every single day. There were countless trips to the corner store, walking three blocks through the alley. One of us kids was always made to go with her to help carry home the beer. I remember feeling angry about all the money that was being spent on alcohol rather than on us. But now looking back, I feel overwhelming sorrow trying to imagine the pain Mom was in and the self-loathing that must have consumed her. There's not a doubt in my mind that she longed to be a better mother—she was just trapped in the throes of an addiction and too depressed to do much about it. Now in my sixties and having lived through my own nightmare, I see things through the eyes of compassion. But this was far from the case when I was sixteen.

By the time I reached high school, I despised my mother. An incident that took place in the 11th grade is very revealing of the condition of my heart regarding Mom. A friend from school invited me and a few other classmates to her church one Friday night for a coffee house, (not that any of us drank coffee or that they even served it for that matter, it's just what we called it back then). During the course of our chit chatting, one of my 'so-called' friends came up with the not-so- brilliant idea that when I went home that evening I needed to tell my mother that I loved her. (*You can't be serious!*) I don't recall what we were discussing that prompted them to make such a ludicrous suggestion. More than likely I was complaining about her (something I often did) and may have even told them that I hated her guts (which isn't always the most Christian thing to say—especially in a church setting). Well, lo and behold, in a matter of minutes every one of my gal pals were in complete agreement that indeed, it was of the utmost urgency for me to proclaim to Mom that I loved her. At first, I tried to blow them off, but they weren't letting up. I began to cry and plead with them, "I can't. It's not true. I'll be struck dead by lightening!" Tough luck for me because the final consensus was, if I was really a Christian, I would do it. (The **suggestion** had thus evolved into a **commandment**—my soul's salvation hanging in the balance, contingent on my obedience.) Well by now I'm sobbing. It was one of those 'deny Christ or face the Lions' moments. After much agonizing, I chose the lions, leaving the coffee house from Down Under (way, way down) to go home and tell my mother the biggest fib of my entire life! When I arrived home, Mom was already in bed and all the lights were out. It took me a few minutes to muster up the strength but finally, choking out the words I mumbled, "I love you, Mom."

Mind you those words were spoken completely void of all feeling and not an ounce of emotion. Nonetheless, I did it.

Well Mom wasn't buying it. She snapped back, "You're a damn liar."

I'm so glad the house was dark because I shrugged my shoulders, breathed a huge sigh of relief and trotted off to bed feeling relieved, as if a hundred-pound weight had been lifted off my chest. My mother was right. I was lying.

While thinking your parents are the most annoying people on the planet is a normal phase that most teens go through, despising them is not. What happened along the way that allowed such dark emotions to infiltrate my heart when it came to my mother? To solve that mystery, I had to do lots of digging into the past in order to understand not just my pain, but Mom's as well.

Mom gave birth to my sister, Lynn in March of 1959. (I was three and a half.) I have a vivid recollection of the day she came home from the hospital. I walked over to my newborn sister, took her little hand and began to shake it.

"Hi Lynn, I'm Robin!" Being a child of exuberant energy, I was more than likely in the process of dislocating her shoulder.

Dad, not in the mood for a trip to the ER, gently scolded me by saying, "Be careful, Rob."

Although I didn't say it, I sure thought it—*Take her back!* From that day on, things were different. Something wasn't quite right in our family. Being so young I'm quite certain I blamed it all on the arrival of my younger sister. Things were pretty good until she showed up. (Well actually they weren't, but what did I know at three?) Still, something was amiss and whatever that something was, it had a profound effect on our mom. She went to her grave never having shared with us what caused her to be so unhappy. Years later when I was doing some inner healing work and trying to piece together events from childhood, I pressed Dad for information. Unfortunately, he couldn't remember that far back. The bottom line is that we never knew what caused the change in Mom. Whatever it was, she plunged into depression which in turn exacerbated her dependence on alcohol. My guess is that she was drinking more in an attempt to numb her pain. Yet in spite of these afflictions, she faithfully fulfilled her motherly duties. There was always food on the table, she kept us neat and clean, doctored us up when we were sick and most definitely made sure we didn't run wild. But the loving mom that was emotionally nurturing—she only showed up every now and then.

As my sisters and I have reminisced about our mother the past thirty years, we are all in agreement that she suffered from Obsessive Compulsive Disorder (O.C.D.) One of the ways it manifested itself was in her need for the house to be tidy. During the evening meal, when Mom was done eating, it was time to start washing the dishes (regardless if the rest of us still had half a plate full of food). If we turned our head to talk to each other, our dish vanished and was whisked off to the sink. Dad once shared with me that when he used to smoke, Mom would wash his ashtray after every cigarette. It annoyed him so much he decided to quit. (*Way to go, Mom!*) When Mom was growing up in the 1930s, no one even knew what O.C.D. was. Even in the 60s and 70s, being labeled with

O.C.D. was a rarity. So, who knew Mom had this disorder? Surely none of us. All I knew from early on was that Mom liked things in place and that a spic and span house made her happy. The reason I share this info on Mom is because a memory from childhood ties into her compulsion and how I dealt with the emotional loss of her.

One day, shortly before my 5th birthday I decided to engage in a cleaning project. My sisters and I had a huge collection of play dishes—plates, cups, saucers and the like that we stored in a doll cupboard. Our modus operandi was to toss them in and close the sliding door as fast as we could before all the dishes came flying out. Needless to say, that little cupboard of ours was a disaster area. So, one afternoon as Mom was lying on her bed, I kicked into high gear and started straightening up and organizing all the stuff we had jammed in that play cupboard. There I was on my knees, right outside of Mom's bedroom, sorting through and organizing 8,436 play dishes. I have no idea how long it took me to complete that task but upon standing up I immediately discovered I had worn two huge holes in the knees of my corduroy slacks (which gives you some idea as to how much energy was exerted into this endeavor). Now granted, I was an energetic little kid but mingled in with all that exuberance was desperation. *Hey Mom, look at me out here cleaning. Doesn't that make you happy? Please Mom, oh, please be happy again.* The simple logic of a four-year-old: *If I make Mom happy she'll come back to us.* Sadly, it didn't work. In time, I stopped trying to win back her heart, which depression and alcoholism had snatched from us.

My dominant love language is touch. Unfortunately, Mom wasn't very 'touchy feely' unless we were being hit or having our hair pulled. Once in a while Grama Zobie would wash our hair and that would put me in heaven (being touched in a way that felt good). I had a friend at church whose mother woke her up every morning with hugs and kisses and when spending the night at her house, I also got showered with all that physical affection. While I wasn't all that crazy about my friend, her mom was the best and I was thrilled whenever I was invited for a sleep over. Our wakeup call was Mom announcing from her bedroom that we needed to get up. That was it. Then at night before we went to bed Mom would say, "Give me a kiss." We would dutifully kiss her on the cheek because, for the most part, we were compliant children. I don't remember Mom kissing me during my school years. Hugs were also a very rare commodity. Grama Zobie was a hugger, as was Dad, and when they were around, I received an abundance of physical affection. But neither of them were part of my everyday life and much like food, sleep and water, I needed a steady diet of loving touches. Did the deficit of physical affection with Mom have an adverse effect on me? Is there a correlation between daughters whose love language is touch and a lack of physical affection from their mothers? Might this be a contributing factor in what leads them into homosexual relations? Most professing lesbians will vehemently deny there is any such cause and effect relationship between the past and the present! I'm inclined, however, to disagree.

As wounded as Mom was, there were times when she morphed into a combination of June Cleaver and Martha Stewart. I have vivid memories of coming home from school to a sparkling clean house, the smell of brownies baking in the oven and a smiling, upbeat mother. On those rare occasions, she was simply amazing and decades later I still feel warmth in my heart reminiscing about the times Mom was everything a kid could hope for. Unfortunately, substance abuse and depression made it all but impossible for her to sustain consistency in being that wonderful mother who showed up every now and then. But there were two days of the year we could absolutely count on Mom being on top of her game—taking a back seat to no one. That was on our birthdays and at Christmas.

When it was our birthday, Mom would make us whatever kind of cake we wanted (as long as it came in a box). She had the ability to make you feel like you were the most important person on the planet when it was your B-day. There was only one year (I think I was 10 or 11) that I remember being yelled at on my birthday and oh boy, did she ever let me have it. Dad, who happened to be over that day and was usually the target of Mom's wrath, got a pass as all her ranting was directed at me. She ragged on me from the time I got up into the early afternoon—hollering at me for just about everything. It all came to a climax when she barked at me to go out to the garage and get something. I don't remember for the life of me what she sent me to fetch, but I do remember high tailing it out of the house just to get away from her for a couple minutes. When I lifted up the garage door, assembled together were all my friends. In unison they shouted, "Surprise!" I turned around and there was Mom, standing behind me in the driveway with a big smile on her face. She had been yelling at me simply to throw me off so I wouldn't suspect anything was up. It was all an act, (for which she could have won an Oscar). I was never more shocked. Well, once the party began, Mom became her usual 'Birthday Super Mom'—spoiling me rotten until I went to bed that night, peaceful and happy. To this day, I wake up on my birthday feeling like the 'Queen of the Universe' and by noon am usually depressed that no one else has figured out just how special I am.

Then there was Christmas. Something about the holidays seemed to alleviate Mom's depression and thus, Christmas really did become the most wonderful time of the year at our house. The decorations were brought down from the attic the day after Thanksgiving and with Mom's supervision our home became a festive, happy place. We decorated our Christmas tree, put out all our Christmas knick knacks and pulled out the holiday sheet music from the piano bench. There were cookies baking in the kitchen and Christmas records playing non-stop in the living room. Although we were poor, we never felt that way on Christmas morning. Even after Dad had moved on, stopped paying child support and ceased being Santa, Mom came through. How she did it, who knows? Yet she made sure we each had a pile of presents awaiting us when we ran to the living room at the crack of dawn on December 25th. But without a doubt, the best Christmas gift of all was having our mother emotionally present and for the most part, happy.

Mom quit drinking my junior year of high school after she was diagnosed with early signs of cirrhosis of the liver. She immediately gave up beer and as far as I can remember, never touched it again. Unfortunately, she continued to hit and yell as, by now, it was a habit. But she did seem to take notice that I was emotionally far, far away from her and thus, she made an attempt to mend some fences. On Friday nights, she would order out food for the two of us to share as we watched the Friday night movie together. As much as I enjoyed the food, I was much too angry to be lured back in by spare ribs and French fries. Sadly, I expressed little (if any) gratitude and remained emotionally unresponsive to her attempts at reconciliation. (*Jesus, could you please tell my mom how sorry I am for being such an ungrateful brat?*)

After I left for college, Mom got it together with the Lord. She began to attend church regularly every Sunday and went to mid-week services as well. God was indeed transforming her life and as a result, our relationship improved. The summer before my junior year of college, I lived with Mom and we often attended church together. It was a difficult season for me as my first homosexual relationship had ended abruptly—leaving me grief stricken. All I told Mom was that my plans had changed and I wasn't going to spend the summer with my friend on the East Coast. She had no knowledge of my struggles with homosexual sin so I did my best to hide that I was crushed and heartbroken. I was certain she would not handle very well the news that I had fallen in love with my girlfriend, so I simply concealed my tears, tried not to mope too much and went to church with her every time the doors were open. However, two years later when I was on the verge of being thrown out of Bible College due to homosexual behavior, I came clean, spilled the beans and found my mom to be a tremendous support. She didn't freak out, yell or ring my neck for getting myself in so much hot water. Instead, Mom arranged for people from her church to come over to the house and do inner healing prayer with me. For sure, the Lord had done a mighty work on my mother (and eventually did one on her daughter as well).

It's taken a long time to admit that growing up with an emotionally detached mother devastated my heart. I believe our broken relationship contributed significantly to my unnatural desires for women (although the decision to act on those desires—that was totally on me). Interestingly, when I was sexually acting out , making the connection between the past and the present was nowhere on the radar screen. It's amazing how sin blinds a person from clearly seeing the obvious—making it impossible to comprehend what's right in front of your nose. Of course, facing the truth can also be very painful (which is why we humans tend to ignore it). But for those who find the courage to do so, there is nothing more freeing. "And you will know the truth, and the truth will set you free" (John 8:32 ESV).

When I began meeting with a Biblical counselor in the fall of 2015, I had for the most part, made peace with the past as far as Mom went. Dad, not Mom, became the focus of therapy. But the Lord in His infinite goodness also provided some missing pieces of the puzzle concerning my mother. Much to my amazement, long lost memories were discovered. Surprisingly, they weren't gloomy ones but rather the kind that fill your heart with love and joy. This gift from God was a direct result of a divine appointment with someone else's mom. Her name was Bernice, but everyone called her 'Mother'.

Chapter 12

MOTHER

I met Mother on October 19th, 2015. I was sitting in a lobby awaiting my first counseling session when she walked in and sat in the chair across from me. We smiled at one another and exchanged hellos. I noticed the bag she was carrying had on it the name of a major Christian publishing company located in western Michigan. I immediately assumed she was a follower of Jesus and that was all the info I needed to strike up a conversation. I began making inquiries about her bag and quickly learned that Mother did editing for that publishing company which prompted me to share that I was a writer and had self-published a book. Naturally, her curiosity was sparked and she wanted to know what my book was about. I spent the next twenty seconds telling her all about my book and she seemed quite impressed (probably not so much due to the content of the book but that I could give her the run down in less than half a minute).

There was something genuine about this woman sitting across from me and in no time at all I felt completely comfortable in her presence. We ended up hanging out together for ten or so minutes which was ample time to tell her my entire life story. She listened intensely with compassion pouring out of her as I unloaded sixty years of baggage right there in the middle of that lobby. As of yet we hadn't introduced ourselves, so I didn't even know her name. But that didn't matter. We had clicked like two peas in a pod and there wasn't a doubt in my mind that we were kindred spirits! When it was all said and done our hearts had bonded, we'd become the best of friends and I couldn't imagine my life without her! We were just about to join hands and sing a verse or two of Kumbaya when my therapist appeared, indicating she was ready to see me.

As it turned out, both Mother and I were there to meet with Dr. Diane Dickinson. I was already so fond of Mother that I was more than happy to have her tag along. Dr. Dickinson (whom I have the privilege of calling Diane) had been one of my college instructors. We had not spoken since I graduated but one Sunday morning, thirteen years later I just so happened to visit the church she belonged to. I had always held her in high regard as she was an excellent teacher so when it became apparent I would have to get into therapy over my Catholic conflict, there was no one else I considered seeing. Well, there we all were, my new best friend from the lobby, Diane, and myself sitting in a little circle. The first order of business was a formal introduction to the woman I had just divulged the depths of my soul to. Her name was Bernice Miree—but I was told that everyone called her 'Mother' (which worked for me as I could never remember anyone's name).

Once the niceties were over, I promptly handed Diane the intake evaluation I prepared in advance so we could get right down to business. She politely thanked me as she looked it over for less than a minute.

Great, I thought, *she can speed read. I might be done with therapy in two weeks at this rate. Thank you, Jesus!*

All was going according to my plans for the first five minutes, and then the wheels fell off the wagon! Dad became the focus of my session and to add insult to injury—it was sprung on me that Mother was going to be my therapist. *NO, NO, NO!* Surely there had been some misunderstanding. I had signed up to be with DR. DICKINSON! Mother seemed like a lovely person, but I had come for information that only Dr. Dickinson would have access to through her vast amount of schooling and research. I needed **her** to tell me why I couldn't free myself from the Catholic Church. I was counting on **her** to give a formal diagnosis (anxiety disorder, PTSD, depression, split personality, just plain crazy) and the three-step solution to fix what ailed me. But my plans had been completely foiled as I was now stuck with Mother and believe you me, I wasn't at all happy about it.

I left therapy in a bit of a tizzy. In my mind, Mother was not up to the task of analyzing the complexities of my life—primarily Catholicism and my messed up relationship with my father. I was ninety-nine percent certain she couldn't cut it but nevertheless, it seemed only fair to at least check her out before firing her. Thank God for the Internet, which allows you to Google people behind their back—allowing you to decide if you want to deal with them or not. Bernice Miree popped right up and admittedly, she was no lightweight. I quickly discovered she was an international speaker, well respected Bible teacher and the founder of a popular women's conference held annually in Metro Detroit. All these things were undoubtedly impressive. But I was looking for specific initials behind her name and coming up empty which confirmed my suspicion. She was not the therapist for me. Besides—I had a degree in counseling psychology and although I wasn't working in the field, I daily analyzed everyone I met in order to keep my skills sharp. Therefore, I needed a counselor that was up to speed and could challenge me (and hopefully do it in a hurry because I was low on funds and therefore needed a very quick fix).

I had thoughts of not even showing up for my session with Mother but in the spirit of Christian charity I decided to give her an hour to prove herself (and then I would fire her, forcing Dr. Dickinson to come back and deal with me). Mother greeted me sweetly, picking up where we left off the week before—bosom buddies (completely unaware that she had since been thrown under the bus). Before we even sat down she commented on my intake evaluation.

"I read the information you wrote up. You're a psychologist."

I was relieved she had figured that out as it would make it easier for her to understand why she was being terminated.

"But," she continued, "your problems aren't psychological—they're spiritual!"

And with that I plopped down on the couch. (*Ouch!*) Mother didn't need an hour to prove herself. In less than a minute she took me out— making it more than obvious she was up for the monumental task of dealing with me. I was actually very relieved.

Okay, cool! Mother's got some game, I concluded. *Yeah, I can do this.* And that was that. I never doubted her again. She was my therapist and it no longer mattered how much money I'd have to dish out. Once she lovingly took my legs out from under me, I realized God was going to use Mother Bernice Miree to heal the areas of my soul that were still a festering mess.

Mother was a straight shooter. Her style was to cut right to the chase and tell me things whether I wanted to hear them or not. I would often deny that what she perceived as the truth was actually correct. She'd hold her ground, though, which would prompt me to start arguing with her. Upon occasion I was even a bit sassy. Many weeks I left pouting, (acting more like a five-year-old than a woman in her sixties). Funny thing, though—I always came back the next week for more, and that surprised me, because I usually disappeared when the things

I wanted to keep under wraps were uncovered and exposed. Perhaps it was her genuine care and deep compassion that lured me back time after time to keep facing the music.

There were many reasons the Lord chose Mother to be my counselor and I believe that one of them was because she spoke my love language. We both experienced and expressed love through touch. The office we met in had two chairs and a couch. I would plop down on the couch and Mother would sit in the chair by a desk, about twenty feet away. But she didn't stay there for long. Each week she would drag her chair over to the couch, so we could hold hands as we opened with prayer. And then she'd stay there the entire hour—inches away from me. Some folks would have found that to be a total invasion of their space. But not me. I loved it. The physical closeness was a tremendous comfort to me and having her right there gave me the courage to deal with painful memories.

Biblical counseling is much different from regular therapy. I wasn't sure what to expect other than guessing it would be Christ centered and involve some Bible verses. I hadn't envisioned there would be praying. (Duh.) But I was cool with it as I love to pray—and praying with Mother was an experience like none other. Around our third or fourth time meeting together, Mother was feeling the Spirit and having a good old Holy Ghost time of prayer. When she came back to the planet she looked at me and asked if I had felt the moving of the Spirit.

"Oh yes, Mother", I replied.

Actually, I hadn't felt much of anything but how could I possibly own being oblivious to a mighty move of the Spirit that had completely engulfed her? I eventually came clean with her (two years later) and fessed up that I had told a fib. While I never quite felt the moving of the Spirit to the degree Mother did, our prayer times began to have a profound impact on me. Oft times I would start crying within moments of her taking my hands. Half the time I didn't even know what was causing the tears to flow. It was almost as if her prayers were plowing away my defenses—exposing the unhealed wounds in my heart and preparing me for the spiritual surgery that was about to take place.

When I was a practicing Catholic I was encouraged to seek the help of the Virgin Mary, the most wonderful Mother of all. I was told that out of her heart flowed maternal love, which would comfort, nurture and soothe any soul that came to her. In the Blessed Mother I would find all that was lacking in my relationship with my birth mother—and then some! By drawing near to her sacred heart and placing myself in her maternal care, she would intercede on my behalf with her Son (which upped my chances for a favorable response to my heart's desire). Wow! That all sounded so good! But of course, I could never go there. No matter how much I needed the love of a mother or how intense my desperation for powerful prayers to be offered up on my behalf, my Protestant roots went too deep to venture down the Mary road. So, I never could accept the offer of motherly love coming from the mother of all mothers. Undoubtedly, many Catholics who knew my story were bewildered and perplexed at my refusal to run into her arms. What was I thinking not capitalizing on such a major perk afforded me as a Roman Catholic? Well, I was thinking it was best for me just to run to Jesus and let Him fill the huge 'Mom hole' in my heart. I wasn't sure how He'd pull it off, not being a mom Himself, but I knew as a 'Scripture-Only' believer I had no other option.

The reason I share that is because one afternoon during therapy, while sitting three inches away from Mother, something amazing occurred to me. God was in the process of filling up the 'mother deficit' I had felt for most of my life through Mother Miree. I had never met anyone more loving, compassionate, nurturing, sensitive and caring than she was. She pampered me when my pain was overwhelming and gently scolded me in moments when I got a little too big for my britches. Her all-encompassing hugs, beautiful smile and hearty laugh brought much joy to a lonely soul that had known too much sadness for far too long. And as far as having a mother who prayed for me? Listen— if Mother Miree didn't have the ear of Jesus, nobody did! Having her become a mom to me was beyond cool—it was a precious gift right from the heart of God.

But as we continued on our journey together down the therapy trail, I came to the realization that God's intent in putting this amazing woman in my life had a higher purpose than just cheering me up. Mother was a necessity to my becoming whole again and here's why.

What made the heartaches, chaos and abuses of childhood so unbearable was the fact that neither of my parents were available to help me cope with whatever crisis I was going through. Dad was physically gone and Mom was far too often emotionally absent. Because of that, I learned at a very early age to shut down emotionally. Mom would often say when we were crying about something, "You better knock it off before I give you something to cry about!" Granted, we were probably crying over something stupid like having to eat our vegetables or being made to wear saddle shoes in the fifth grade (which was social suicide back then). But that wasn't always the case.

When I was about thirteen years old Mom had a boyfriend named Allen who lived in Virginia. He came up to Michigan for a visit and I totally fell in love with him. Already by then I suffered with severe abandonment issues and the night Allen was saying his goodbyes to return to his home, I totally lost it. I was sobbing uncontrollably because another man I loved and wanted for a dad was leaving me. Did my mother attempt to comfort me? Unfortunately, no. She yelled at me to stop crying. I eventually learned to stuff my pain so far down that I couldn't attach appropriate emotions with horrific memories from childhood. Theophostic helped a great deal when it came to reconnecting feelings with the specific trauma that had occurred. I did plenty of crying during those sessions and was never told by Ann and Trisha to "get a grip!" Ann, though only four years my senior, was in many ways also a surrogate mother to me. She was understanding and non-judgmental, which created a safe environment to feel my pain. Hanging out with Mother was all that and then some. I now had another mom in my life who was committed to helping me uncover more dark secrets from my past. I knew that Mother Miree loved me and because of that, I felt secure enough to deal with things I had been running from for decades. It was okay to sob in her presence without fearing she would tell me to stop crying. (Not even a chance of that ever happening.) One afternoon as I sat on the couch directly in front of Mother, with tears streaming down my cheeks—she reached out and gently wiped my tears away with her fingers. I will forever be comforted by that memory.

Because therapy has time constraints, there were weeks the session ended before I regained my composure. In other words, I sometimes walked out the door while coming apart at the seams. If an old, infected wound was uncovered, an hour was rarely enough time to process everything. I would drive home feeling miserable, depressed, raw, exposed and just a little peeved that Mother would send me off in such a condition! But what she knew, and what I would soon come to realize, is that I wasn't on my own. Amidst the distressing emotional excavation I was undergoing, two words from Isaiah 9:6 came to life: "Wonderful Counselor." Being omniscient, the Lord was able to show me the connection between the pain I was feeling and the historic event that was feeding it. There were weeks I left therapy not knowing why I felt so awful and what I was even crying about. Mother was really good at connecting the dots if I gave her enough information. But I couldn't always remember what happened as I had spent too many years pushing things out of my consciousness. Jesus, however, knew all of my story. He also knew my heart's desire for truth, so He was more than willing to whisper things to me not only during my quiet time but even when dusting my apartment or out walking the dog.

Just as amazing as His omniscience was, the Lord also gave me a new understanding of His omnipresence. I was only able to hang out with Mother for an hour a week. But the One called "Emmanuel" was with me 24/7, never sleeping or slumbering (Psalm 121:4). He was right there in the middle of the night if I woke up crying or just needed a friend to talk to. During my waking hours He walked behind me and before me, all the while with His hand laid upon me (Psalm 139:5). As cool as Mother was, no way could she pull that off. His Spirit not only lived in me (2 Timothy 1:14) but I also lived in Him (Acts 17:28). For years I wondered how that was even possible. But if God is in every molecule of air, every drop of rain and every ray of sunshine, then all those verses are more than beautiful imagery. They reveal absolute reality. At long last it was starting to sink in that God not only had knowledge of every painful thing I went through in my life because of His all-knowingness, but He also knew every detail of all my moments on earth because He went through them with me. How amazing is that? And what a big, fat liar the devil is, who told me again and again that I was all alone and nobody gave a rip.

So that's how it was—Mother would tenderly remove old, dirty bandages that had been plastered over past hurts for decades and then the Great Physician would take it from there—cleansing those wounds and sewing me back up. Needless to say, this part of therapy—wound lancing and debridement was hard, painful and no fun at all. So one week, needing to lighten things up a bit, I brought my photo album to my session and did 'show and tell' with Mother. Turned out she was the perfect person to share those pictures with as she did major fussing over every photo.

"Ooh, weren't you adorable?" she asked me with emotion just gushing out of her.

There were pictures of Mom, Dad, my grandparents, siblings, and me. Those photos began at birth and went well into my twenties. When we came to the pages in my photo album of myself with Mom, something very strange began to happen. There was a picture taken of my mother pregnant with me, about a week before I was born. Mom was holding a birthday cake for my older sister who was turning four. (Our birthdays are eight days apart.)

When Mother saw that photo and said to me, "Look at how your mother is glowing. Do you see that?"

Truth be told I had never really noticed—so I took a closer look. *Well, I'll be!* Mother was right. Mom was absolutely beaming with joy. *How'd I miss that?*

Mother continued to see and comment on the obvious. When she saw pictures of Mom holding me as a newborn baby she said,

"Look at how she's gazing at you with so much love in her eyes."

I focused my eyes on those photos as if seeing them for the very first time. There was no denying it—my mother was already crazy about me.

"Can't believe I never noticed that before," I sheepishly confessed.

Our parents took lots of pictures of us when we were little. Mom dressed us in matching outfits and we looked so cute you'd have thought we were on our way to costar in a Shirley Temple movie. When Mother saw those pictures, she immediately picked up on something that I once knew but had long forgotten.

"What treasures you girls were to your mother!" she exclaimed.

For all the times I had thumbed through my photo album as an adult, it hadn't occurred to me that I was valuable and precious to Mom. But hearing Mother's words awakened my memory to a significant event from my mother's childhood.

When Mom was a child, she, my aunt and the neighborhood kids would entertain themselves by stealing ice from the neighborhood ice truck. Why they did that, I never thought to ask. Perhaps it was just for the thrill of doing something they weren't supposed to do and the challenge of not getting caught. Whatever the case may have been, during one such crime spree, Mom fell, and the truck backed over her—crushing her pelvis. The doctors told my grandmother she would never have children. But the Lord, ever merciful, cancelled that prognosis by blessing her with three daughters. Those old photos revealed how she felt about us—proclaiming loud and clear, "Look at my three little miracles!"

As I sat on the couch next to Mother, staring at those pictures from yesteryear, God opened my eyes by allowing me to see what I had been blind to for most of my life. And once my eyes were opened, I experienced a miracle of my own. I once again remembered being loved by her.

Even after Mom stopped drinking, when things became much better between us, my heart was still so wounded I couldn't connect with her on an emotional level. But there I was, many years later—feeling loved by the Mom who once held me in her arms. That afternoon my soul was reunited to the mother I had before her afflictions took her away from me. This reawakening was beyond anything I could have imagined or hoped for. It wasn't even on my list of things I was praying for. (*Dear Lord, could you take me back to age three and let me feel Mom's love once again?*) It never occurred to me to ask for this. So, I guess you could say I was blindsided (in a wonderful sort of way). Mother and I weren't doing any serious digging into the past when this moment arrived. Good grief—we were just looking at old pictures and having a light-hearted time of it. But that day the Lord gave my mother permission to proclaim from the other side, "I LOVE YOU!"

Okay—I know that's not Biblical. But that's exactly what it felt like. Well, however it happened, I was reconnected to my mother's heart of love and the memory of her love has remained with me every day since.

Mother Miree played a big part in reawakening my heart to the love of my mom. God used her nurturing, maternal heart to help me remember that once upon a time my soul was saturated with mommy love. Being in her presence week after week reminded my soul what a mother's love was like and because of that, my heart woke up to a beautiful reality. I had a mom who loved me.

Many times I expressed my gratitude to Mother for all of her insights, kindness and mostly for showering me with her love. Mother's response was always the same. It went something like, "It's the Lord who deserves all the glory."

She said it much more elegantly, but that was pretty much the gist of it. I understood what she was saying and almost felt as if I had just blasphemed the Holy Spirit by giving Mother His due. And yet I couldn't stop expressing how much I appreciated her and how grateful I was that she was there for me.

After about the fourth time she told me, "All the credit goes to Jesus," I finally had a comeback for her. (Alright—so I'm a little slow.) "Yes, Mother—but you availed yourself to Him. You seek the Lord constantly, study His Word diligently, pray unceasingly and all those things make it possible for God to touch and bless others through you. So thank you, Mother. From the bottom of my heart I am very, very grateful."

Having said my piece, Mother simply smiled and nodded. I smiled as well. I continue to smile, though my weekly get-togethers with Mother have long since ended. She's always close in spirit and will forever have a special place in my heart.

And to think I almost fired her! Oy vey! I am so glad the Lord doesn't let me call the shots.

Chapter 13

GENDER IDENTITY CONFUSION

A while ago, Facebook decided to give folks the option of customizing their gender when setting up their profile. At last count, there were fifty-six choices. Here's a few of them: 'Gender Queer', 'Gender Questioning', 'Bigender', 'Cisgender', 'Gender Fluid', 'Intersex', 'Neither', 'Other', 'Trans', 'Two-Spirit'. Soon thereafter I decided to delete my account as an act of protest, with a prayer that thousands of my brothers and sisters in Christ would follow suit decrying, "ENOUGH ALREADY!" Sadly, that didn't happen, and Facebook lives on to encourage perversion and support everyone's right to be as deranged as they want to be.

I often wonder what it must be like to grow up in the world in which we now find ourselves. Although the sixties were far from perfect, things seemed more clear cut. Granted, the boundaries were being tested, balked against and in some cases, beat down. But for most of my growing up years, the gender issue was non-negotiable. Like it or not, you were stuck with what was typed on your birth certificate. That, however, is no longer the case—which leaves me wondering if I should retake high school biology. I barely got through it in 1970, struggling to pull off a C minus (and that was with only two genders to learn about). Being tested on fifty-six of them would have undoubtedly been the undoing of me. The one thing I had down pat—males being XY and females XX, is now completely obsolete. Chromosomes no longer determine one's gender; feelings do. Hmmm—on second thought, biology might be a cakewalk for me this time around, seeing how there's no longer correct answers to memorize. It appears you now get to make it up as you go along. (*Heaven help us!*)

Although I may have had an easier time in science classes, growing up in today's world would have been very harmful for me as I was a gender confused child. Had changing my gender been an option when I was sixteen years old, I shudder to think what my choice would have been. Most, if not all gender confused individuals claim they have been put in the wrong body. They either don't believe in the God who created them, or they view Him as a total moron who doesn't know what He's doing. Or perhaps like me, they make up who God is and how He operates. When I was into New Age thought, I was convinced that my gender confusion had to do with reincarnation. I concluded that in my most recent past life I had been male. Although I chose to reincarnate as female, my soul still felt a very strong connection to that prior existence which resulted in my masculine identity and my inordinate attraction to women. At the time, this made perfect sense to me. But I now realize it was simply an indication of how disturbed I was! After repenting, God in His mercy began restoring my mind. Needless to say, I've now reached a much different conclusion as to what caused my gender confusion.

I can't recall a time from childhood when I was your typical female. Though Mom dressed me in identical dresses to match my older sister, my outer appearance was not reflective of my inner reality. One Christmas our parents bought us beautiful, life size dolls. When Annie (my big sis) opened hers, she began to cry because the leg had fallen off her doll. I opened mine and wanted to cry because they had given me a doll! (What were they thinking?) A couple years later, Santa brought us a huge doll house. Now that, I loved—but only because you could send the plastic people down the staircase on their backsides and watch them fly right into the swimming pool. What a blast!

Strangely though, I did like Barbie. Annie formed a Barbie fan club with all the neighborhood girls and made me a charter member. We were seriously devoted to Barbie which motivated us to do more than sit around, talking about how cool it was to have a Barbie doll and be part of her fan club! Nope—not us! Someone came up with the brilliant idea that we should design our own line of Barbie clothing and get one of our moms to do most of the work. Our plan worked and at a meeting soon thereafter each of us was presented with a very stylish green corduroy coat for our doll. All that was left to do was sew on a couple of buttons. Though I had never done any sewing before, how hard could it be to sew on a couple of buttons? I put my all into this task—sewing with a vengeance. Upon completion, I stood up proudly announcing, "I'm all done!" only to discover I had sewn the coat to my skirt. (*Oh, good grief!*) That was that. I immediately lost all interest in Barbie, dropped out of our little fan club and focused my energy where I excelled: playing ball.

Football, basketball and baseball were activities I could engage in from morning till night. The boys in the neighborhood usually let me play baseball with them as they were often short of players and I could pretty much hold my own. Annie would sometimes play catch and shoot hoops with me in our backyard and for a girl, she was pretty good. But eventually she lost interest in chasing after balls and decided chasing after boys was much more fun. I missed playing catch with her because that meant I'd have to throw a rubber ball against the back of our house and play catch with myself.

Whenever there was a pick-up football game in the neighborhood, I was ready for action. Most of the time the boys weren't all that eager to include me but after a fair amount of begging on my part they'd relent and bring me into the huddle. I felt so confident in my ability to go head to head with the fellas on my block that I played tackle football with them until I was in the ninth grade. My football career came to an abrupt end when one afternoon I was leveled by a NFL style hit—knocking the wind right out of me. Fortunately, it also knocked some sense into me. Though I loved the game as much as they did, I had to concede the fact that guys were bigger and stronger and if I wanted to keep walking and breathing, my football days were over.

When I was growing up, girls like me were referred to as tomboys. For many gals this was nothing more than a phase of adolescence that most eventually transitioned out of. Had my home environment been healthier, it's likely I would have done so as well. But things being what they were, that would not be the case for me. When Dad left, Mom put on me most of the household tasks he once took care of. Yard work became my job. Putting up storm windows in the fall and screens in the spring was my responsibility as well. In autumn, I raked the leaves and when the snow fell, I was out shoveling it. My ability to repair things was right up there next to my sewing skills so I was spared from becoming the family handyman. But almost everything else Dad did—if I had the know-how and ability to complete the job, it ended up on my list. Thus, my masculine identity was enhanced.

While cross-dressing has been around for centuries, I had no knowledge of such a thing during my growing up years. There were well defined standards that dictated what was gender appropriate. Most of us willingly submitted to the guidelines without questioning if they were fair, oppressive or infringing on our rights. If you were female, you dressed like one. We not only wore dresses to church but to school as well. However, once the seventies hit, the rules we'd been playing by began to loosen up, be rewritten and in some cases, eliminated all together. In 1970, our school district made the decision to change the dress code—permitting girls to wear slacks to school. (*Yippy Skippy!*) The new school policy did not permit anyone to wear blue jeans but we couldn't have cared less. We had been liberated from skirts, dresses and pantyhose. We were euphoric and our bliss knew no limits (nor did our unruly behavior). Girls could now leap over chairs, sit on top of counters in the science lab and do most everything the guys did as we no longer suffered from the constraints of dreadful, feminine attire. Eventually, the churches got with the program and women began showing up for Sunday worship in pant suits. Unfortunately, these changes did not bode well for me as there was now no place that required me to put on my girl clothes and thus, I became all the more removed from my female identity.

Many have argued that gender identity confusion and homosexual behavior are unrelated but for me, that wasn't the case. Both were so deeply intertwined it's difficult to know for sure what came first and which issue fed the other. I can see where gender confusion could have easily bred my homosexual desires. The more I lost touch with being female and replaced feminine traits with masculine characteristics, the more I felt drawn to women in ways that were inappropriate. The feelings I should have had for boys, I had for girls. Sadly, I had no idea what was going on with me. I really wanted to have a boyfriend but very few guys found a boyish girl all that attractive. The only school dance I attended was Sadie Hawkins, as the gals asked the guys to go with them. Even then I had to ask half the school before someone finally said, "yes".

When I decided to attend Bible College in the fall of 1975 and found out there was a dress code requiring female students to wear feminine attire, I had a mini meltdown. First of all, at this stage of my life I had no girl clothes. Furthermore, the school was located in Minneapolis and they couldn't be serious about women walking around campus in January with nothing on their legs but stupid nylons! But after the shock wore off, I hitched a ride on over to Kmart in search of skirts which I dutifully wore for the two years I was there. Once I graduated, it was back to slacks. Interestingly, I did go through a phase about twenty years later where I once again wore skirts, dresses and even high heels. I was referred to as a 'lipstick lesbian'. I cannot recall what possessed me to do such a thing but nevertheless, I morphed into quite the little lady. But still being an active, unrepentant homosexual sinner, nothing had inwardly changed. I had simply whitewashed the tomb in which I resided. Eventually this phase ended and all the feminine clothing I had been parading around in was donated to the Salvation Army. Soon thereafter, it was back to guys' pants, men's shirts (which were six sizes too big for me) and novelty ties loosely hanging around my neck. I continued to wear make-up but only because it made me look better.

(More about vanity than a desire to be feminine.) When I started attending Mass in February of 2009, every article hanging in my closet had been purchased from the men's department. Only after repenting and doing a significant amount of inner healing did a legitimate transformation occur that was genuine and lasting.

In former times, the general consensus when helping a gender confused individual (specifically those walking away from homosexual sin) was to immediately deal with the outer appearance. Perhaps the reasoning was that if the outside changed, the inside would follow suit. I understand, and maybe for some folks this is a good strategy. But it may backfire and send people running in the opposite direction, so I'm not totally convinced this is the best place to start. In my case, gender confusion was not only an outward reflection of inner turmoil, it was also a defense system—put in place to protect myself from further harm.

In part, gravitating towards male activities came about because I was so close to my father. As Mom became less available, both physically and emotionally, my need to connect with Dad intensified—resulting in my acting more like a son than a daughter. But that's not the whole story. I'm convinced that as I observed my mother suffer abuse at the hands of an angry man, I rejected my female identity so Mom's fate would never become mine. My mother was the epitome of femininity. She was soft, gentle, tender, beautiful and completely helpless when it came to defending herself against my father's physical aggression. There was no way I wanted to be like her or ever find myself in a similar situation. If this is what it meant to be female, then I wanted no part of it! Taking on a boyish persona became my way of projecting toughness and letting others know not to mess with me. Of course, underneath the surface I was scared of everyone but I wasn't about to let that cat out of the bag. This was my way to shield and protect myself from being hurt. And after being molested by some neighborhood boys, that shield was reinforced even more. The end result was further disconnection from my God given identity—making me all the more aligned to a masculine facade.

In light of that, I was ever so grateful no one tried to tear down my walls in the early days of the recovery process. Perhaps folks wanted to, but instead, I was given freedom and liberty to wear whatever I had hanging in the closet. I felt accepted and loved no matter what outfit I had on and that gave me time to experience a good amount of internal healing. Once that happened, I felt safe enough to dismantle the outer shell and allow the woman inside to come out of hiding.

After Unbound, Shepherd's Group and Theophostic, I had mended to where the body cast of masculinity I'd been living in could be removed. My wardrobe that consisted of male attire was replaced with articles of clothing purchased from the women's department at JC Penney's and Sears. In time, skirts and dresses once again occupied the hangers in my closet. My gal pals gave me lots of positive affirmations when

I showed up at church looking like the woman God created me to be and I truly did appreciate every single kind word. But when my guy friends told me I looked nice—it put me on cloud nine! After a lifetime of put-downs from members of the opposite sex, their kind, affirming words were like a sweet balm on a soul that was still raw and tender.

As I became more attached to being female, I began to find much delight in the presence of men. It tickled me when they held open the door or offered to carry my stuff. I began feeling safe in their presence—seeing my guy friends as protectors rather than assaulters. That for me was a real turning point. I found myself more desirous for the protection of a man than the comfort of a woman when life threw curve balls at me. That may seem insignificant and have some of you shrugging your shoulders but it really was monumental. It let me know that God had done some major healing in my heart.

The Lord has brought me to a place where I now joyfully accept my God-given gender. I am truly grateful He created me female. Am I a rare anomaly or is the healing I experienced available to others? While it does appear that I have been the recipient of mega amounts of God's unmerited favor in that He went to great lengths time and time again to rescue me and bring me back into the flock, I have a very strong suspicion He's wanting to do the same for others. I realize that there are folks out there dealing with greater challenges regarding their gender, due to physical and genetic abnormalities. In all honesty, I don't have the answers for these complicated cases. But even in such situations, the Lord is still sovereign and totally in control because after all, "…he is God: it is he that hath made us, and not we ourselves" (Psalm 100:3a KJV). "Thy hands have made me and fashioned me" (Psalm 119:73a KJV). "For you created my inmost being; you knit me together in my mother's womb" (Psalm 139:13 NIV). So, whatever the case may be, God is not up in Heaven pacing back and forth, trying to figure out what in the world went wrong. Whatever your story, the Lord knows exactly who you were created to be.

Only God can bring about deliverance from the gender insanity whirling all around us. My constant prayer is that we, the people of God, will not cave in and start waving the white flag of surrender (as many have done on the homosexual front). As a church we need to pray for a fresh outpouring of the Holy Spirit to embolden us to once again unapologetically proclaim the truth. Will there be push back? Undoubtedly. Might we be blasted on social media, lose three-hundred of our Facebook buddies and be called every name in the book in order to discredit us? You can most definitely count on that. Will folks, sympathetic to the transgender community, leave our churches, (taking their checkbooks with them)? My guess is that, yes, they will—and that's probably a serious concern for many pastors (explaining in part why so few seem to address this issue). Whatever price we may have to pay, God has called all of us who bear His name to stand up for the truth. Jesus came to save, heal and restore sin-sick sinners through the power of His transformational love. If in the process of fulfilling this mission we offend some, annoy others and just plain get on everyone's nerves, so be it. Gender Identity Confusion (as I have so named it) **is** a disorder and the consequences are all to often devastating. It puts folks at odds with the One who made them and completely robs them of the God ordained life they were created to live.

May God give us the courage to stand for truth and the faith to act on that which we claim to believe.

Chapter 14

IN SEARCH
OF A FAMILY

I've often heard it said that parents who don't get along and are at each other's throat constantly should divorce as it is better for the well-being of their children. I contend it's actually better if they get some help, learn to get along and save their marriage. Several chapters ago I let the cat out of the bag that my mom and dad could get pretty crazy at times, exposing their daughters to frightful scenarios. Nevertheless, for me there was nothing better than being a family—all of us together in one house, living under the same roof. I really and truly loved that. I wanted both of them there when I fell asleep at night and when I woke up in the morning. Having two parents in my life every day was something I counted on and needed to feel safe and secure. Of course, it's not like I was verbalizing these sentiments at age five. Yet somehow, in my heart, I knew this was the way things were meant to be: a mom, a dad, and their offspring, living with one another as a family unit, day after day, month after month, year after year.

Our mother was a stay-at-home-mom and that meant she was with us 24/7 until we started school. Dad went off to work Monday through Friday but faithfully returned home to us each night (which was the best part of my day). His job required no out of town business trips nor did he work any overtime. Like clockwork he pulled in the driveway at 5:30 p.m. each weeknight and shortly thereafter we would sit down as a family to eat dinner. Weekends belonged to his girls. Dad didn't go off on fishing expeditions or golf getaways with his buddies. He worked around the house and then did fun things with his daughters. One Saturday morning he made us chocolate waffles. We thought that was beyond amazing and concluded we had the coolest dad on the planet! He was steadfast in driving us to church each Sunday morning and bringing us back home a couple hours later—where we once again gathered around the table as a family to eat a fabulous dinner Mom had prepared. But then one day, the car stopped pulling in the driveway. There was an empty chair at the table where our father once sat. The car was gone, Dad was missing, and my joy was no more.

I'm not sure I would have survived childhood if not for the Baptist church I attended from 3rd grade until I left for college. Because I was sinking in a sea of sorrow, I grabbed on to that church like a drowning person latches on to a life preserver.

It became a feeding trough for my starving soul and a shelter from life's turbulent storms (of which there were many).

"I was glad when they said unto me, Let us go into the house of the Lord" (Psalm 122:1 KJV). That sentiment was in my heart long before I knew it was a verse from the Bible. "Better is one day in your courts than a thousand elsewhere" (Psalm 84:10 NIV). Truth be told, there was no place I would rather have been than at church. If I fell sick on Sunday or a church activity night, I would cry and beg my mother to let me go anyway. During my High School years when Mom deemed I had done something worthy of punishment, she would ground me from going to church. For many high schoolers, going **to** church would be appropriate punishment. But not for me. She had figured out that the best way to make me suffer for whatever crime I had committed was to deprive me of what I loved most. Indeed, missing church was torture to my soul.

One of the best treasures of childhood was belonging to a church that was within walking distance. The church was less than a half mile from our house so we could make it on foot (even in a blizzard). I would often stop by the church on my way home from school, even though it was several blocks out of the way. There were many days I needed to talk to our Christian Education Director Mrs. Ruthie so I gladly hiked the extra distance. Mrs. Ruthie's door was always open and as busy as she was, I never felt hurried off or as if I was bothering her. She had a way of making me feel like she had nothing better to do with her time than to listen to whatever was on my heart. We actually kept having the same conversation over and over again—me complaining about my mother and Mrs. Ruthie replying that Mom had many problems so I should try to be understanding. (I was a total loser when it came to being empathetic.)

My childhood church hosted a full slate of activities. Sunday morning, of course, was the worship service with Sunday school immediately following. Sunday afternoon we had youth choir rehearsal followed by the Sunday night church service. Wednesday night was Quest Group, a small group Bible study that met in various homes. When I was in the 9th grade some of the older kids formed a Christian folk group called, The Crusaders. They practiced on Thursday nights. Loving to sing and loving to hang out at church, there was no way I wasn't joining this group. Friday evenings I attended Canteen (a three-hour social for the youth). It alternated each week between the junior and senior high kids so that meant two Fridays a month I was home with Mom watching movies and eating French fries. Add to that a roller-skating party on the first Tuesday of every month. Our church rented out an entire roller rink and folks from every age group came out to skate. Not being much of a skater I spent most of the evening sprawled out on the floor. It didn't help that I was trying to keep up with my friend, Judy, who was the Peggy Fleming of the roller rink. Nevertheless, it was a total blast and well worth the thirty bruises I woke up with the next morning.

But of all the activities our Baptist church hosted, my very favorite was the annual church picnic held at an amusement park called Boblo. The park was located on Boblo Island and the only way to get there was on the Boblo Boat with none another than Captain Boblo at the helm. The first thing we did after landing on the island was eat. It was the one day of the year where our parents allowed us to gorge on ice cream 'til it was seeping out of our pores. Once we were completely buzzed on sugar, the grownups got ditched. We all took off to ride the rides until our hair stood on edge and our eyeballs were popping right out of their sockets! Oh, the fun we had racing around that island, having the absolute time of our lives. It was a marvelous day of exhilarating fun and I still light up like a Christmas tree many years later, reminiscing about running wild on Boblo Island with my friends from church.

I could go on and on about the good old days at Redford Baptist church, but I've more than likely gone on far too long as it is. I am, however, fighting the urge to spill the beans about Camp I Dare You and how every year Mrs. Ruthie roamed about in her nightie with a big flash light in hand, searching high and low for all the naughty campers who had snuck out of their cabins in the middle of the night. "Kids— come on now. Let's all get back inside," she'd whisper, trying to not wake up the law-abiding campers who were sound asleep on their bunks. It was indeed hilarious! But then again, perhaps you had to be there to appreciate how truly funny it was to be playing flashlight tag at 3 a.m. with the pastor's wife. Okay… moving on.

The reason for this journey down memory lane is to convey that church was my lifeline. It patched up the gaping hole in my heart caused by the breakup of my parents' marriage. I was there almost every day of the week and while that may indicate an obsession or perhaps even a religious addiction to some of you, I believe it was an innocent attempt to find an everyday connection with people I loved, replacing what I once had with my father. The more I spent time with the folks at church, the more it felt like being part of an intact family and oh, how I needed that. Dad was gone and my Mom had her hands full just trying to stay afloat. At church I found surrogate parents who hugged me, encouraged me, built me up and gave me a sense of worth. No wonder I wanted to be there seven days a week. Doesn't every child need a steady stream of love coming from their parents?

Once I went off to college, things were never the same. I'd attend church when home for the weekend but, no longer being part of the everydayness of church life, I was out of the loop and therefore felt disconnected. Most of my friends had also gone off to school and many of the families I had been close to had up and left our congregation. Things had even changed between Mrs. Ruthie and me. Although she never stopped caring, her time and energy were being invested in the kids that were around week in and week out. I'm certain she continued to pray for my soul but the days of her chasing after me with a flashlight were over. It was time for me to move on and find a new support system within another local church. Unfortunately, I never did. Oh, there were times I made an attempt to engage with a local body of believers—but the more entrenched I became in homosexual sin, the less likely it became for me to relate to anyone in a healthy fashion. Sadly, I never lasted anywhere more than six months (if that). Somebody would hurt my feelings, slight me, offend me or tick me off, and that would be it for that congregation. I would quickly move on to the next house of worship to do this routine all over again. That went on and on, year after year, decade after decade. And then... I became a Catholic.

Blocking out so many painful memories from childhood made it difficult to connect the dots between the present and the past. I was completely oblivious to what force was drawing me into Catholicism. People would often ask me, "With all your objections to Catholic doctrine, what made you want to join?" I don't think I ever gave a very good explanation to that question because truth be told—I didn't know why. It would take leaving the Church and spending many hours sitting in Jesus' presence before I finally understood what had pulled my heart into a religious system whose doctrine I could never fully embrace.

Catholicism brought to light a key component of who I am. I am an everyday sort of person. Pure and simple, I need daily connection. As a child, I counted on Dad to come home every night. Just as there was a physical need to eat food each day, emotionally I needed his presence in my life, Sunday through Saturday, fifty-two weeks a year. My stability and emotional well-being depended on that. When my father stopped showing up each night, a gaping hole was left in my heart. For many years my childhood church plugged up that hole—keeping me afloat. However, once I went off to college and no longer had a church connection, I tried to satisfy the need for daily connectedness with a female partner. That game plan though tried again and again, ended badly each and every time. After repenting I walked away from homosexual relating and ran right into the big, strong arms of the Roman Catholic Church. Depending on your view of Catholicism, that may seem like another ill-advised move on my part. Be that as it may, God used it to do amazing things in my life.

In a previous chapter devoted to Catholicism, I left unanswered what made the Catholic Church irresistible to me. What deep seeded need in my soul did Catholicism meet? Why did I feel powerless to resist the tug on my heart to enter in? Was it the rituals, the gorgeous cathedrals and the beautiful spirit of reverence Catholics exhibited at Mass? Was it the sacraments? Did I feel drawn to this church because it had been around for two-thousand years, affording me the much needed stability my life so sorely lacked? While all those things were an absolute treasure to me, none of them were what really drew me in. It wasn't until months of therapy with Mother—talking week after week about Dad—and as I said a moment ago, it wasn't until hours on end of being in the presence of Jesus that I finally had an 'Ah ha' moment. The light went on and I understood that which had mystified me. The Catholic Church gave me back the everyday connection I once had with my father.

Being Catholic grafted me into a whole new family, led by men I called 'Father'. Mass was the place where my spiritual siblings and I daily gathered to dine at the Lord's table. It was at the Eucharistic love feast that I had a genuine feeling of belonging—the same feeling I knew as a child and had long forgotten (yet constantly sought after). And even though weekday Mass was brief in duration, I always left satisfied. Singing songs, praying, hearing a brief homily and receiving the Eucharist filled my heart with enough joy to sustain me throughout the day. And the best part of all was that I could do it all over again the very next day!

I know that sounds so trite, elementary, completely unspiritual and you can't believe you read this many pages anticipating an earth shattering revelation only to have me say this. Granted, it would have been much more holy of me to declare it was receiving Jesus at the altar that drew me in. I'm very sorry to have disappointed you but the goal here is to be truthful—not impressive. While Holy Communion was something I dearly loved and sorely miss, especially seeing how most Protestant churches only celebrate the Lord's Supper once a month, for fear it will become too mundane, it wasn't what compelled me to become Catholic. My soul had been searching for a day-to-day connection with people I loved and belonged to. A family! I don't know if this is true for everyone but the best thing about being part of a family for me was having regular, consistent connectedness and knowing I could count on it. This is exactly what I found in the Roman Catholic system.

Although I didn't attend Mass every day, I often went four to five times a week. But even when not at church, my Catholic friends were close by. Many of them lived in the neighborhood and I had total freedom to pop in whenever I needed a hug or to just connect for a few minutes. Having those spontaneous get-togethers felt like family and I will forever be grateful for the open doors that welcomed me unannounced. It was as a Catholic that I regained the inner security I knew as a little girl—attending a neighborhood church where the doors were open every day. When the parent I most counted on was no longer on the scene, that Baptist church surrounded me with love. And then many years later, having walked away from the hope of forming a family with another woman, the Catholic Church was there to welcome me into the biggest family on the face of the earth. Protestants have no idea what that feels like because we've become so fragmented and isolated from one another. Most of us belong to a single church that has its own selection of songs, own worship format and oft times even their own spin on the Scriptures. (*Lord, have mercy on Your children!*) Catholicism, however, is under the same canopy. Granted, some in the tent are bending the rules a bit (perhaps even a lot). But still—the Mass is the Mass everywhere you go and because of that you have a sense of belonging to every Catholic Church on the planet. I for one really loved that because like I said, I'm an everyday person and in Catholicism I found constant, consistent connection—365 days a year.

Since being back amongst the Protestants I have often brought up how great it would be to have the church doors open every day, where folks could gather, sing a song or two, pray for one another and break bread together. In my perfect world, evangelicals all over town would congregate for daily fellowship. Unfortunately, my pleas for daily gatherings have for the most part fallen on deaf ears. (Perhaps they heard me but considered my suggestion so ridiculous there was no point in acknowledging I was even talking.) The few who have taken the time to respond to my ludicrous idea kindly tell me just to seek God on my own and let Him meet the needs of my heart by developing an intimate relationship with Jesus (as if I wasn't doing that as a Catholic). While that is a helpful admonition and something I fervently adhere to, it's not the way the early church operated. (Surprise, surprise, surprise!)

When Jesus taught His disciples to pray, one of the things they were to ask for was "daily bread" (Matthew 6:11, Luke 11:3). Some will argue He was talking about having our physical needs met each day and while that is a correct interpretation, it appears the first century believers (led by the apostles) took it to mean even more than that. "And they, continuing daily with one accord in the temple, and breaking bread from house to house, did eat their meat with gladness and singleness of heart" (Acts 2:46 KJV). "And daily in the temple, and in every house, they ceased not to teach and preach Jesus Christ" (Acts 5:42 KJV). Were these new instructions the first century Christians received after Pentecost, via special revelation from the Holy Spirit? Or were they simply continuing in the footsteps of Jesus who for three years was daily in the temple—teaching, preaching and healing (Matthew 26:55, Mark 14:49, Luke 19:47&22:53)? I have a strong suspicion they already had this routine down pat.

I will forever miss the daily connection available to me via the Catholic Church. The twice-a-week-get-togethers with the Protestants on Sunday morning and Wednesday night feels too much like visitation with Dad, who had us Sunday afternoon and took us midweek to the drug store for ice cream. Catholicism was salve on a very old soul wound, caused by the loss of my everyday Dad. The joy I felt being in the Catholic Church for six years brought great healing to my heart. And yes, when I walked away the bleeding resumed—but fortunately it wasn't the hemorrhaging I experienced as a child. I am learning that God's grace is sufficient even when the family institutions He ordained, biological and spiritual, fall short. His children are everywhere. They live in my apartment building; I work with them and pretty much meet them everywhere I go. It's not the same bond I had with my Catholic compatriots but it's enough to remind me I'm still part of a family—the family of God.

Nonetheless, I will always be an advocate for returning to the New Testament model of gathering daily. Whether anyone in a position of authority ever agrees with me and chooses to do something about it remains to be seen. So, until then, I'll just keep on whining about how much I miss being Catholic and remind my Protestant brothers and sisters on a regular basis that, in regard to how often the early church met, the Roman Catholics are more Biblical than Protestants. Perhaps that will one day get their attention. Then again it may get me a one-way ticket to the local nunnery.

Chapter 15

THE WONDER
OF SALT

Having undergone a major transformation by the grace of
God obviously changed everything for me. For starters,
the joy and bliss I felt were off the chart! I was finally at peace
with God (after being in a category five hurricane for most
of my life). I was full of zeal and excitement—on a mission
to share with everyone how good it was of God to rescue me
from the muck and the mire. And from the deepest part of
my heart there came a desire to see others experience the same
freedom from that which is robbing them of life. But as the
years have passed, I must confess, discouragement sometimes
plagues my heart. I know it's a sin on my part to succumb to
it because it dampens my joy. And yet everywhere I look I see
broken lives in desperate need of healing who live in hopeless-
ness and despair. I believe with all my heart that God wants
to restore them. Sadly, I find fewer folks who are wanting to

jump on this bandwagon with me. Is it because we lack faith? Or is it because we lack salt?

For the record—I really like salt. As far as I'm concerned, food without salt is dreadful. Unsalted peanuts? (I don't think so.) Saltless potato chips? (Oh pleeze!) Salt free popcorn? (Gag me with a spoon.) No salt on my sweet potato fries? (Don't be ridiculous!) Salt adds pizzazz to food. It takes a bland, boring dish that not even our dogs will touch and has us going back for seconds. Salt affects the taste of every edible thing it encounters. Mashed potatoes, scrambled eggs, pasta or a juicy steak. (Pass the salt!) Can you imagine corn on the cob without salt? (No way, no how!) Who knows? Perhaps the Jews would have done less complaining in the wilderness had God dropped down some salt shakers along with the evening quail. (On second thought, probably not.)

In ancient times salt was a highly valued commodity. Salt was used by the Egyptians to preserve mummies. Roman soldiers received part of their pay in salt. The Latin phrase, *salarium argentum* was known as 'salt money'. Long before self-defrosting Kenmores appeared in every home, salt was used as a preservative. Meats were packed in salt to prolong and prevent the rotting process (caused by the growth of bacteria). It is believed that during the Civil War, some Northern generals implemented a strategy to deprive the South of salt. Not only did that mess with their food supply, it also effected their horses who needed salt in their diet. General Sherman ordered one of his captains to be put on trial for aiding the enemy because he allowed salt to pass through the Union lines to the Confederate troops.

In Old Testament times salt was used in worship. According to Leviticus 2:13, "You shall season all your grain offerings with salt. You shall not let the salt of the covenant with your God be missing from your grain offering; with all your offerings you shall offer salt" (ESV). Salt was required for all of their offerings because it represented the people's commitment to the covenant. Ezra 6:9 includes salt as one of the items in the temple offering and Ezekiel makes mention of salt being cast upon burnt offerings (Ezekiel 43:24). Numbers 18:19 and 2 Chronicles 13:5 both refer to "a covenant of salt." While there are no other verses in the Old Testament clarifying what exactly a covenant of salt was, commentators believe it was an agreement or contract between God and His chosen people, Israel, that was unchangeable—even in the midst of their fluctuating circumstances.

Salt's healing benefits have been utilized for centuries. It is recorded in 2 Kings 2:19-20 that Elisha threw a bowl full of salt into a spring of bad water. The result: "Thus says the Lord, I have healed the water" (2 Kings 2:20a ESV). Of course, added to the salt was the miraculous power of God but I find it significant that He used a natural resource that already had healing properties in it. Ezekiel 16:4 infers that newborn babies were rubbed with salt to promote good health. And speaking of health—long before Antiseptic Wipes could be purchased at Walmart or on Amazon, salt was used to cleanse wounds. Even now, centuries later, after all of our medical advancements, salt is still doing its thing. Navy seals have reported that being in saltwater speeds up the healing of their gashes. Folks with aching muscles, swellings, inflammation and sprains are still soaking in Epsom salt. Is there anything better when dealing with a sore throat than to gargle with warm saltwater? I think not.

Unfortunately, salt in our current culture has lost its luster and prestige. In the opinion of some, it's right up there next to arsenic! It has contributed to so many health issues that some restaurants have removed it from tables. One must now beg and cry for a saltshaker and sign a disclaimer that if you stroke out in the middle of your meal, you promise not to sue! Truth be told, while iodized salt may still be useful for gargling, it's not the wisest choice to put on your fries. Pink sea salt, on the other hand, contains 84 essential minerals required by the human body so it's actually good for you. (How cool is that?!)

"You are the salt of the earth, but if salt has lost its taste, how shall its saltiness be restored? It is no longer good for anything except to be thrown out and trampled under people's feet" (Matthew 5:13 ESV). The disciples of Jesus more than likely got it. I imagine they were actually quite blown away when He said that seeing how they were living in a time when salt had great value. We, on the other hand read, "You are the salt of the earth" and conclude that analogy is no longer relevant as we are in the process of being delivered from our saltshakers. But what we really need to be delivered from is our salt aversion. Fact: the call to be salt still applies two thousand years later. Like it or not, a 'low sodium' church is ineffective, and a 'salt free' church is just plain worthless. (His words, not mine.) All three synoptic gospels implore us to remain salty because once we lose our saltiness, well, it seems we've got a bit of a problem. Again, (in case it didn't sink in a moment ago) Matthew 5:13 states, "You are the salt of the earth. But if the salt loses its saltiness, how can it be made salty again? It is no longer good for anything, except to be thrown out and trampled underfoot" (NIV). Mark's gospel reiterates what is written in Matthew, but the words of Jesus recorded by Luke paints an even grimmer picture. "Salt is good, but if salt has lost its taste, how shall its saltiness be restored? It is of no use either for the soil or for the manure pile. It is thrown away. He who has ears to hear, let him hear" (Luke 14:34-35 ESV).

As much as I like salt on my food, the salt analogy Jesus used was not one that I gave a whole lot of credence to. I was more enamored with being "the light of the world" (Matthew 5:14). Shining brightly for Jesus appealed to me. But being salt? Not so much. It wasn't until after researching and pondering all the wonderful benefits of salt that I had a sodium awakening! Now I lget it. Perhaps because I was so messed up and wounded, I've been able to really appreciate why Jesus needs His church to be salty. Truth be told, if not for some faithful servants of the Lord who took their salt commissioning seriously, I would not have experienced a whole lot of healing (if any).

How wonderfully good God was to bring just the right folks into my life who were committed to the preservation of the Gospel message. They consistently proclaimed that the same Jesus of Scripture who set captives free, delivered folks from darkness and radically changed lives, was still operating in like manner two thousand plus years later. They were unabashedly not ashamed of a gospel that demanded repentance from sin and complete obedience to the One who purchased us at Calvary through the shedding of His blood. Sadly, that's not the most popular message these days. Nonetheless, they stayed the course, remaining faithful to the timeless, eternal truths found in His Word.

I remain ever indebted to and grateful for the friends in my life who told me the truth about myself even when their words stung my soul. I knew that the truth would set me free (Jn. 8:32) but I wasn't planning on it hurting so much in the process. Of course, I was anything but grateful in the moment of these confrontations. (There's an understatement for you.) I behaved much the same way I did as a little girl when my mother was applying Merthiolate to a scraped knee. That stuff stung like crazy. It was dreadful and I absolutely hated it. My younger sister Lynn, the 'Google Whiz', did a little research and discovered there was sodium in Merthiolate. (Sixty years later—mystery solved!) Yes indeed, that's exactly what salt does. It stings! But it also cleanses which is why my mother inflicted that pain on me and why my friends, decades later, loved me enough to do the same.

Yet amidst the stinging and all my whining, there was plenty of soothing. Ann does this very cool thing she refers to as 'soaking'. She will sit next to someone, gently touch their arm or shoulder and quietly pray in the Spirit. I'm not sure where she came up with that, but it certainly is a great application of being the salt of the Earth. Just like good old Epson salt soothing my aching muscles, God has used Ann to soothe my broken, wounded soul by soaking me in love. How interesting that salt is used to both sting and soothe. As the salt of the Earth we are called to tell the truth and then soak folks in love. Truth and love—both equally part of our salt calling.

Being the salt of the earth is something unique to the Lord's Earthly children. Angels do not share this characteristic, nor does Scripture mention this being one of God's attributes. This is our gig and ours alone. While that may seem like no big deal to some, I find much meaning in it. Though God's Word will stand forever (Isaiah 40:8), we have been given the task of preserving its potency. And while God is the ultimate healer, He has equipped us to assist Him in ministering to others on the road to recovery, applying the necessary salt to both cleanse and soothe souls in need of healing.

When the Lord gave us new life in Christ and sealed us with His Holy Spirit, part of our spiritual DNA included this valuable commodity: S A L T! **This** is our calling and our assignment. Most of all, it's our great privilege. We are the salt of the earth. It's us or it's no one. We have been given what is needed to carry out the ministry of reconciliation. Jesus has equipped us to be His instruments—aiding in the restoration of others. Only one thing needs to be decided: will we believe this is indeed the truth? I have done my very best to convince you. All that's left to say is this: I dare you! **Dare to Believe!**

Made in the USA
San Bernardino, CA
19 February 2020